50

IDEAS YOU REALLY NEED TO KNOW

ISLAM

MONA SIDDIQUI

Quercus

Contents

Introduction

Today, no other world religion is under as much focus as Islam. Whether regarding issues around the headscarf and religious freedom or Islamic State and militant extremism, Islamic thought is at the centre of much public and political debate. And yet, despite the public, and often controversial visibility of Islam – especially since 9/11 – millions of Muslims live ordinary lives as ordinary citizens in Muslim and non-Muslim countries. Whether they are secular, practising or non-practising, their lives are connected in multiple ways to the rituals of prayer and fasting, to mosques, madrasas, to laws on marriage and family life. There is no one way to be a Muslim as Muslim societies and civilizations are rich and varied.

This book explains the major terms and themes associated with Islam. While many of these ideas can be found in introductory books on Islam, the *50 Ideas* format provides succinct chapters on a hugely varied array of theological, literary and sociological terms linking historical and contemporary analyses. All selection is to some extent subjective and reflective of personal choice and style. However, I have tried to bring together those subjects that one would expect to find in such a book – the Qur'an, *hadiths*, the Kaaba, Sunni/Shi`a – while discussing more complex debates around Islam and human rights, gender, democracy and pluralism. These should not be seen as postcolonial Western concerns, rather they are intrinsic to how Muslim societies are rethinking and reimagining the very soul of Islam in the 21st century.

Mona Siddiqui

Presentation and Acknowledgement

For ease of reading, I have avoided using diacritics in transliteration of mostly Arabic words. The format of Qur'anic verses cited here is chapter first followed by the verse(s), for example Q33:40. I would also like to thank my doctoral student and research assistant Mr Josef Linnhoff for his invaluable help with some of the ideas and the text as a whole. I have learnt that a book that looks simple is probably one of the hardest, yet most imaginative things to write!

01 Allah

For Muslims, belief in an omniscient creator and merciful God is the fundamental tenet of one's faith. The Qur'an, the primary religious text of Islam, is God-centred; the 'I' or 'we' in the Qur'an is God speaking. God is the creator, God is judge and God is mercy. Through the act of creation, God expresses all three of these attributes. These are are just three of ninety-nine such attributes, or names of God (*al-asma al-husna*), but they are all premised on the fundamental belief that God is One. This is the essence of Islamic monotheism or *tawhid*.

The Arabic word for God is *Allah*. The Qur'an repeats at least 30 times, 'There is no God but him', and has multiple ways of relating the oneness, the munificence and mercy of God. In fact, the *shahada* itself – the witness to faith that is the basic creed of Islam – claims: 'There is no god but God and Muhammad is the messenger of God' (see Chapter 10). Many of the Qur'anic verses offer short and eloquent descriptions of this unity. See, for example, 'He is God, [who is] One. God, the eternal refuge. He neither begets nor is born, nor is there any equivalent to him' (Q112:1–4). God's oneness cannot be compromised. *Tawhid* is the central idea that ties all the other themes together in the Qur'an and volumes have been written about the meanings of *tawhid*. The beginning, the middle and the end of the Qur'an and much Islamic thought suggest different avenues for exploring this most pervasive, yet elusive, essence of Islam.

TIMELINE

14,000 BCE	MID-1ST CENTURY CE
Birth of monotheism	Birth of Christianity

GOD'S WILL

In Muslim theology, God speaks throughout the Qur'an. God speaks to man in different ways during the course of human history and, in revealing the Qur'an, he reveals not himself, but his will. The Qur'an refers to God's mode of revelation as inspiration (*wahy*) – that he does not reveal of himself directly but 'from behind a veil' or via the sending of messengers. It is God who has given us life, it is God who will cause us to die and God who will then raise us again from death. Nothing is impossible for God, for it is he who gives everything its place and order. He has only to say 'be' and it is.

GOD'S IMAGE

We can try to imagine God, but as the Qur'an says, 'No vision can grasp him, but his grasp is over all vision: he is above all comprehension, yet is acquainted with all things' (Q6:103). Yet God wishes to be close to his creation so that he is 'closer to man than his jugular vein' (Q50:16). The Qur'an also speaks of God's hands, God's face, God sitting on a throne. In Muslim thought, God is both so very near and yet so completely transcendent and

Allah – what's in a name?

The word 'Allah', according to several Arabic lexicons, means 'the Being who comprises all the attributes of perfection'. Thus, the word denotes perfection and knowledge and the best qualities. This meaning is supported by the Qur'an when it says, 'His are the best (or most beautiful) names' (Q17:110; Q20:8 and Q7:180). Many Muslims use the word Allah interchangeably with God, yet the word itself has long been used by Christians in reference to God, and in those parts of the world that are now predominantly Islamic, but have not always been so. In other words, the word Allah predates Islam.

Malaysia is religiously and culturally diverse. In 2013, a Malaysian court ruled that non-Muslims could not use the word Allah to refer to God, even in their own faiths, overturning a 2009 lower court ruling. The appeals court said the term must be exclusive to Islam, even though people of all faiths use the word Allah in Malay to refer to their Gods. The two million Christians in Malaysia argued that they had used the word, which entered Malay from Arabic, to refer to their God for centuries and that this new ruling violated their rights. Many argued that this was a political ploy by the governing Malay-Muslim party, UMNO, to boost its Islamic credentials. Not all Muslims supported the ban and many Christians said they would continue to use the word Allah in their worship.

7TH CENTURY	7TH CENTURY	12TH CENTURY
Birth of Islam	Islam arrives in southern Asia	Islam spreads to South East Asia

unknowable, that these concepts present a theological challenge. Perhaps the most beautiful words about God are:

> Allah is the Light of the heavens and the Earth. The example of his light is like a niche within which is a lamp, the lamp is within glass, the glass as if it were a pearly [white] star lit from [the oil of] a blessed olive tree, neither of the east nor of the west, whose oil would almost glow even if untouched by fire. Light upon light. Allah guides to his light whom he wills. And Allah presents examples for the people, and Allah is knowing of all things. (Q24:35)

GOD'S MERCY AND HIS LOVE

If we look carefully at creation (see Chapter 11) and observe the beauty and symmetry found in nature, this is itself a sign of divine mercy. God is *al-Rahman*, the most merciful and this mercy is the overriding attribute of God, even when we disobey, when we are ungrateful or when we do wrong. In fact, God's merciful and forgiving nature is mentioned over 500 times in various ways in the Qur'an.

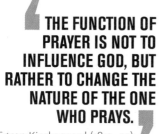

THE FUNCTION OF PRAYER IS NOT TO INFLUENCE GOD, BUT RATHER TO CHANGE THE NATURE OF THE ONE WHO PRAYS.

Søren Kierkegaard (1813–55)

The Qur'an is replete with exhortations to man to observe nature, to turn to God, to desist from denial of God and disbelief (*kufr*), so as to avoid the punishment of the hereafter. And the Qur'an also says that God will forgive humankind all their sins, except the sin of ascribing a partner to God (*shirk*):

> Allah does not forgive associating anything with him. But he forgives other than that as he wills. But the one who associates with Allah has indeed strayed far away. (Q4:116)

Yet, in another verse, it would appear that even this can be forgiven:

> Say, O my servants who have transgressed against their souls. Do not transgress against the mercy of Allah for Allah forgives all sins. He is oft-giving, most merciful. (Q39:53)

For many Sufis on their mystical path, love of God is the highest in rank and the last stage in drawing towards God before repentance and patience. Love is not a means to God, love is the end station (see Chapter 41).

GOD'S PRESENCE

Most Muslims are aware of God's presence in their daily life through the constant remembrance of his name. There are multiple traditions that encourage remembrance of God (*dhikr*), simply by saying Allah repeatedly. This occurs, not only in ritual worship such as in the saying of prayers, but also in many ordinary

occurrences. For example, it is common to say 'Praise be to God' after sneezing, 'May God reward you', instead of thank you, or 'MashAllah' – as God wishes – when witnessing or hearing good news about someone. These phrases are part of the everyday language for Muslims and remembrance of God through these phrases is not necessarily regarded as an extra act of piety, but as normal speech in everyday conversation. In this way God's name is kept alive in peoples' hearts and minds.

In many Muslim households, it is also very common to see plates, ceramics, frames and wall hangings with the words 'Allah' and 'Muhammad' written on them in Arabic calligraphy. For the faithful, these serve as a protection from evil and a reflection of God's presence.

The condensed idea
No one person or religion owns God

02 Muhammad

Islam's central character is Muhammad. With a number of descriptions, including 'messenger of God' (*rasul Allah*), 'the blessed Prophet' (*nabi karim*) and 'God's beloved' (*habib Allah*), Muhammad is not just any prophet in a long line of historical prophets, rather he is the Prophet, the last chosen prophet to be the recipient of the last divine revelation.

Muhammad is referred to in the Qur'an as the 'seal of the prophets' (*khatam al-nabiyyin*), generally understood in Islam to be the final messenger after whom no more messengers or prophets will follow. 'Muhammad is not the father of any of your men, but he is God's messenger and the seal of the prophets.' (Q33:40) For Muslims, he embodies the perfect messenger and the perfect man. Such is the reverence for Muhammad in Islam that Muslims rarely mention his name without adding the words 'and peace be upon him' often shortened to 'pbuh'.

MUHAMMAD'S ROLE

The concept of prophecy is shared between Judaism, Christianity and Islam, though the significance of prophecy varies in each religion. The Islamic view is that prophets and messengers throughout history act as bridges between God and the temporal world. It is in the receiving of God's communication that humankind understands something of God, a God who both hides and reveals of himself. Prophets and messengers are central to God's plan and all of his messengers from Adam to Muhammad have brought the same primordial truth: the oneness of God and human obligation to worship God.

TIMELINE

570 CE	622 CE
Birth of Muhammad	Prophet's *hijra* (migration) and building of the mosque in Medina

The Qur'an is concerned with both individual prophets and the nature of prophecy in the dialectic between human reception and divine message. In that sense, Muhammad is the same as previous prophets. He can only speak of that which is part of God's plan and can only reveal that which God wishes him to reveal. His task,therefore, is to reveal the new truth but not to contest the old truths nor to distinguish between the messengers who preceded him:

> The messenger has believed in what was revealed to him from his Lord and so have the believers. All of them believe in God, his angels, his books and his messengers saying, 'We make no distinction between any of his messengers', and they say, 'We hear and obey and we seek your forgiveness O Lord for to you is the final destination'. (Q2:285)

THE BIRTH OF ISLAM

While the Qur'an often speaks to Muhammad directly, it is not a biography of the prophet. Most biographical accounts of Muhammad's life go back to the text of Ibn Ishaq, a Medinan scholar who compiled the first full biography, or *sira*, of Muhammad, called *Sirat Rasul Allah*. Written a century after Muhammad's death, this biography comes to us through the works of a ninth-century scholar named Ibn Hisham, who edited Ibn Ishaq's texts.

On the basis of early Muslim sources, it is said that Muhammad's father died around six months before Muhammad's birth in Mecca and so he was brought up by his grandfather, Abd al-Muttalib of the Banu Hashim clan of the tribe of Quraysh. At the age of six, his mother Aminah also died. Now an orphan, Muhammad was raised by his uncle Abu Talib, the most powerful man in Mecca. Muhammad gained a reputation for reliability and honesty as he grew older and, in 591 CE, this attracted a proposal of marriage from a woman called Khadijah. A wealthy widow, some 15 years older than Muhammad, she was involved in

632 CE

Prophet dies leaving
no successor

c. **730 CE**

First written *hadiths*
(sayings of the
Prophet)

Images of Muhammad

Islam's central prophet is the prophet Muhammad. In daily conversation, it is common to add the letters 'pbuh' after his name, meaning 'peace be upon him'. While Muslim thought has never divinized Muhammad, he retains a sacred place in the hearts and minds of many.

In recent years, there have been several displays of anger from a number of Muslims who felt that the Western press had attacked the Prophet. The Danish newspaper *Jyllands-Posten* published cartoons of the Prophet on 30 September, 2005. Twelve caricatures of Muhammad were printed in the paper, accompanying an editorial criticizing self-censorship in the Danish media. Not all of the cartoons showed Muhammad, yet one portrayed the Prophet standing on a cloud, holding back a line of smouldering suicide bombers trying to get to heaven. Muhammad is saying, 'Stop stop, we have run out of virgins' (a reference to the tradition that Muslim martyrs are rewarded with virgins in heaven). Another cartoon showed Muhammad as a would-be terrorist, carrying a lit bomb in the shape of a turban on his head. Fury over the cartoons, among hundreds of Muslims, led to protests, arrests and a number of deaths.

In 2015, the French satirical magazine *Charlie Hebdo* was the target of a terrorist attack in which 12 people lost their lives, including the magazine's publishing director Charb (Stéphane Charbonnier) and several other cartoonists. This attack was seen as a response to several controversial cartoons that had featured the Prophet.

the caravan-camel trade. Khadijah supported Muhammad fully and was the first to accept his message which became known as 'Islam'.

In 610 CE, when Muhammad was around 40 years of age, he began to withdraw to the outskirts of Mecca to mediate. It was during one of his meditaions, in the cave of Hira, that Gabriel came to him and asked him to read. What Muhammad read became the first revelation of the Qur'an. From 610–32 CE, Muhammad continued to receive revelations that were oral in nature – that is, they were words spoken to him or words that he found in his heart and then uttered. The phenomenon is described as follows:

'Messenger of God, How does the revelation come to you?' The messenger of God replied, 'Sometimes it comes like the ringing of a bell: it is the hardest on me. Then it passes from me after I have grasped what it said. Sometimes the angel appears to me like a man. He speaks to me and I grasp what he says.'

From the very first revelation when Muhammad is told to recite, the Qur'an then addresses Muhammad by words such as *qul* (say). It is to Muhammad that God reveals the recitations and it is Muhammad's role to spread the message he receives to his tribespeople, the Quraysh, and then the rest of Meccan society. It is Muhammad who, after the migration to Medina in 622 CE (see Chapter 3), eventually establishes what Muslims perceive to be a small Islamic state that subsequently expanded rapidly to make Islam a world religion.

PROPHETIC PRACTICES

As Muslims made Muhammad the focus of the ideal life, it became imperative to know exactly how he lived and what he said. His life and words became encapsulated in the concept of *sunna*, a word that originally related to the habits, customs and practices of any community, but subsequently came to be associated with Prophetic precedent alone.

IF GREATNESS OF PURPOSE, SMALLNESS OF MEANS AND ASTONISHING RESULTS ARE THE THREE CRITERIA OF A HUMAN GENIUS, WHO COULD DARE COMPARE ANY GREAT MAN IN HISTORY WITH MUHAMMAD?

Alphonse de Lamartine, *History of Turkey*

The development of the Prophet's *sunna* was a gradual process for the Muslim community and was reflected in reports and sayings attributed to Muhammad, which became known as *hadiths*. Numbering in their thousands, these *hadiths* are distinct from the words of the Qur'an. Despite centuries of debate and discussion around the status and validity of *hadiths*, they remain a primary lens through which to understand Muslim devotion to Muhammad. *Hadiths* also became the second most important source of authority after the Qur'an, informing all kinds of social, legal, moral and ethical questions about Islamic life (see also Chapter 35).

The condensed idea
Muhammad's message is the same as that of other prophets – worship one God

Hijra

The most common meaning of *hijra* is 'migration'. For Muslims, the word *hijra* encapsulates Muhammad's migration from his home town Mecca to the city of Yathrib, later named Medina, in 622 CE. This date marks the beginning of the Muslim lunar calendar. It also marked the beginning of the reshaping of the Arab peninsula, both politically and socially.

In purely physical terms, the *hijra* was a journey between two cities approximately 320km (200 miles) apart from one another. Prior to the *hijra* of 622 CE, there is also the *hijra* of 615 CE, when a group of Muslims fleeing Meccan persecution at the hands of the Quraysh, arrived at the court of the Christian king, the Negus in Ethiopia. Muhammad did not emigrate on this occasion, but did leave Mecca in 622 CE, in order to avoid assassination and preserve his community. He and his followers sought a stable base in Medina where they could worship in peace without fear for their lives. Although the Qur'an does not narrate the story of this migration, it is structured around the event. The chapters (*suras*) of the Qur'an are divided between the revelations Muhammad received in Mecca and those he received in Medina; in common parlance, they are referred to as 'Meccan verses' and 'Medinan verses', respectively.

MIGRATION, FAITH AND COMMUNITY

Muslims see this time of Muhammad's migration as a new beginning, ushering in the birth of a new civilization. It introduced a quasi-revolutionary spirit of brotherhood within the disparate groups of migrants

TIMELINE

615 CE	622 CE
The first *hijra*; Muslims flee persecution to King Negus in Ethiopia	Muhammad's migration from Mecca to Yathrib (Medina)

(*muhajirun*), who had left their homes and possessions to support the nascent Muslim community in Medina. The Qur'an makes reference to this migration:

> Indeed, those who have believed and emigrated and fought with their wealth and lives in the cause of God and those who gave shelter and aided – they are allies of one another. But those who believed and did not emigrate – for you there is no guardianship of them until they emigrate. And if they seek help of you for the religion, then you must help, except against a people between yourselves and whom is a treaty. And God sees what you do. (Q8:72)

Travel for the sake of God features frequently in the Qur'an. It points to the collective efforts made by groups leaving the comfort and tranquillity of their homes 'in the way of God' to those who welcome them for the sake of God. New relationships and bonds of friendship emerge as a consequence of migration where the migrant and the traveller must always be provided for. This theme is often discussed in the Qur'an. References to both the emigrants and those who helped them in Medina convey the strong bond that emerged through faith, migration and community. People left their homes in Mecca to follow the Prophet in Medina, while those who helped them in the new city spent of their own wealth giving shelter and aid.

These helpers were the *ansar*, notably members of the two Medinese tribes, the feuding Al-Khazraj and Al-Aws whom Muhammad had been asked to reconcile before leaving Mecca. These tribes formed new alliances and came to be his most devoted followers. Medina also had three significant Jewish tribes: the Banu Qurayza, the Banu Qaynuqa and the Banu Nadir.

> **PERHAPS TRAVEL CANNOT PREVENT BIGOTRY, BUT BY DEMONSTRATING THAT ALL PEOPLES CRY, LAUGH, EAT, WORRY AND DIE, IT CAN INTRODUCE THE IDEA THAT IF WE TRY AND UNDERSTAND EACH OTHER, WE MAY EVEN BECOME FRIENDS.**
>
> Maya Angelou
> (1928–2014)

20TH CENTURY	2014
Mass migration from across the Muslim world to the West	Islamic State urges global Muslims to make *hijra* to the self-declared caliphate in Iraq and Syria

The Constitution of Medina, a rudimentary document trying to establish a political order, said that Jews who allied with Muslims were to be part of this new *ummah* or brotherhood.

THE REFUGEE EXPERIENCE

Both the Bible and the Qur'an offer various stories on migration and its being a refugee experience in which one is forced to leave one's home owing to poverty, violence or other threats. For example, Abraham is forced to leave his father's house and Moses flees from Egypt in the middle of the night with his people. In fear of Herod's soldiers, Mary and Joseph seek refuge with the infant Jesus. Finally, Muhammad's own *hijra* to Medina is an example of the centrality of the refugee experience for God. Travellers and migrants are seen as two distinct categories of people with specific needs, but the Qur'an often blurs the distinctions between them. It does so, because both groups of people are vulnerable or uprooted in some way. As in many civilizations and traditions, travel has long been romanticized as well as extolled as a noble activity in the pursuit of knowledge and for creating new horizons.

Over the centuries, *hijra* has come to mean, not just physical movement, but reimagining ways of being a better Muslim. In the early modern period, with the Muslim expulsion from Spain, and then the devastating effects of colonization, as well as the more recent displacements of peoples such as the Palestinians, *hijra* has assumed a new poignancy. It is a constant movement between forgetting the past and keeping it alive. The concept of *hijra* has become a spiritual exercise helping people to hold onto hope in the face of exile, homelessness and loss.

Today, the militant group known as Islamic State (IS; also Islamic State of Iraq and Syria (ISIS) or Islamic State of Iraq and the Levant (ISIL)) has given *hijra* a new militarized meaning for the purpose of their own mission. *Hijra* must be about physical movement, a call to arms, a new jihad (see Chapter 47) against any opposition and especially the West. This *hijra* is not about individual search or peaceful coexistence in new lands. For groups such as IS, the term is invoked to lure people to their violent cause and to convince

Travel literature

The Qur'an and *hadiths* give little account of the different types of traveller, but travel is important for Muslim self-expression and once formed an essential part of nomadic desert life. Travel narrative was an expression of Arab identity, especially during the pre-Islamic period. Poetry served as the medium through which pre-Islamic ideologies were transmitted to the wider population. Poetry both informed the collective consciousness of the people and was memorized as part of the culture of nomadic ideologies.

A major theme of the pre-Islamic ode is the telling of a poet's journey by horse or by camel. It was in this context that the poet could give an account of his adventures in the wilds of the desert, and related the various difficulties he experienced along the way.

In the post-Islamic period, the traveller could be both the migrant and the pilgrim hoping for both rational and spiritual transformation. Three famous travellers are Ibn Jubayr (1145–1217), Ibn Battuta (1304–68/9) and Ibn Khaldun (1332–1406). Travel was a means of recording history and those who travelled carried ambitious aims, to cover as much land as possible and to survey different cultures in all their richness.

other Muslims that migration to their new caliphate is a moral and religious duty on all. This is the message of their leader, Abu Bakr al-Baghdadi, who calls on Muslims to migrate to Syria and Iraq to help build the Islamic State.

The condensed idea
Migration can be an escape and a search

04 Mecca

Mecca is the heart of Islam. It is where Muslims go to perform *hajj* (pilgrimage). As the birthplace of the prophet Muhammad and the site of the Kaaba, it is the spiritual capital of the Muslim world. All Muslims pray in the direction of Mecca, known as the *qibla*, and so the global Muslim community is both physically and spiritually orientated towards Mecca throughout its daily life.

Surrounding the Kaaba is *al-masjid al-haram* (the Sacred Mosque), the largest mosque in the world, but Mecca was a sacred city long before the emergence of Islam. According to Muslim belief, the Kaaba was originally built by Adam and repaired by the prophet Abraham after it was damaged during the flood of Noah. This religious history is alluded to in several Qur'anic verses. Muslims believe that Mecca had already been a place of pilgrimage and trade for the Arab tribes in the pre-Islamic period, although during this time Mecca had become a centre of idol worship. Many of the shrines of the idols that were worshipped across Arabia were housed in Mecca, in and around the Kaaba. The ruling clan of Mecca, known as the Quraysh, enjoyed a prosperity that was based on annual pilgrimages to these shrines. On this basis, Muslims see Muhammad as re-establishing Mecca as a sacred city and the primordial centre of monotheism, following the precedents of Adam and Abraham.

MUHAMMAD'S MECCAN PERIOD

Mecca is primarily sacred for Muslims as the setting of much of the Qur'anic revelation. The first 13 years of Muhammad's prophecy, during which he lived

TIMELINE

570 CE	610 CE	622
Muhammad born in Mecca	Muhammad receives first revelations in the Cave of Hira, a few miles outside Mecca	Muhammad and early Muslim community forced to flee Mecca and arrive at Yathrib or Medina

in Mecca with his followers before the emigration to Medina, is called the 'Meccan period'. Throughout these Meccan verses, the Qur'an typically focuses on central theological topics such as the nature of God, the Last Day of Judgement and the reality of heaven and hell. It also critiques the injustices and malpractices of Meccan society – the accumulation of wealth (Q104:2-3), the failure to treat the needy (Q90:12-16) or the prevailing practice of female infanticide (Q81:8-9).

Arguably the most distinctive feature of these verses is how the Qur'an frequently reassures and comforts Muhammad. The picture we receive throughout the Meccan verses is of a prophet deeply grieved by his rejection by much of the community:

> Perhaps [Muhammad] you would kill yourself with grief that they will be believers. [But] if We willed, We could send down to them from the sky a sign for which their necks would remain humbled. (Q26:3-4)

> And be patient, [Muhammad], and your patience is not but through Allah. And do not grieve over them and do not be in distress over what they conspire. (Q16:127)

This is perhaps the great paradox of Mecca. While it became the holiest city in Islam, for a long time it was also a bastion of opposition to Muhammad. It was in Mecca that the Prophet suffered increasing persecution over the course of 13 years, before eventually fleeing to Medina. While Muslims today revere Mecca as the birthplace of Muhammad, some of his fiercest opponents were also children of the city, including the Quraysh and his uncle Abu Lahab, named and condemned in the Qur'an. It

> ONE OF THE GREAT PUZZLES OF EARLY ISLAMIC HISTORY IS THE SHEER UNLIKELINESS OF WHAT ACTUALLY HAPPENED. A THOUGHTFUL ARAB LIVING IN THE ARABIAN PENINSULA A SHORT TIME BEFORE THE CONQUESTS WOULD HAVE HAD EVERY REASON TO LAUGH OUT LOUD AT THE SUGGESTION THAT ARABS WOULD SOON BE WORLD RULERS, REPRESENTATIVES OF A NEW UNIVERSAL FAITH AND PURVEYORS OF A VIBRANT CIVILIZATION.
>
> Daniel Brown, *A New introduction to Islam*

629 CE

Muslim conquest of Mecca

20TH CENTURY

More than 15 million Muslims visit Mecca annually for various pilgrimages

Message in Mecca

The central Qur'anic concept – the unicity of God – is known in Islam as *tawhid*. Preaching the message of the oneness of God to the Meccan community was the Prophet's biggest challenge. Not only did it demand that the Meccan idolators physically destroyed their existing idols, but also that all other religious communities should adhere to the truth.

Monotheism existed prior to the advent of Islam but polytheism, in the form of worship of idols, spirits and other beings, formed a great part of the Arabian religious landscape. The pre-Islamic period of Islam, known commonly as the *jahiliyya*, is important, not only for understanding the context in which Islam emerged, but also because it is very often referred to as the period that stands in contrast to everything Islam brought.

The Islamic message, as contained in the Qur'an, essentially discusses a new way of thinking about this world and, perhaps more importantly, about life beyond this world. This thinking demands first and foremost a rejection of the multiple gods that the Arabs could see and worshipped for the sake of the one true God whom they couldn't see but who was the Creator of all.

It is perhaps hard to imagine today, just how revolutionary this idea was for those who couldn't quite grasp why they should give monotheism any credence; essentially, why should they worship one god because a person of relatively little significance told them to do so?

was these Meccans who continued to do battle with the Muslim community throughout the Medinan period, until the Prophet's eventual victory and successful return to Mecca in the year 632 CE. It is also worth noting that after this conquest the Prophet returned to, and remained in, Medina until his death. It was Medina, not Mecca, that was the capital of the early Muslim empire, and it remained so until the Caliph Ali moved the capital to Kufa, in southern Iraq, in 656 CE.

MODERN-DAY MECCA

Recent decades have seen arguably the biggest and most sudden period of change in the history of Mecca. The rise of affordable plane travel means ever-increasing numbers of followers can now finance the *hajj* pilgrimage. As a result, the Saudi authorities have undertaken a massive process of expansion and development within the city. This includes a near-constant expansion of the holy mosque to accommodate more worshippers.

These developments have been controversial, however. Much of Mecca is now a city of steel and glass, all luxury hotels, skyscrapers, fast-food outlets and designer boutiques. Most controversial of all has been the construction of the *Abraj al-Bait*, also known as the Fairmont Makkah Clock Royal Tower. The third-largest building in the world, this comprises a luxury hotel and shopping mall and is situated directly in front of the holy mosque and Kaaba. Many see the modernization of Mecca coming at the expense of its sacred character. Critics also point out that little of the history of Mecca remains, as the expansion of the city has led to the destruction of many historic buildings that date back to the time of the Prophet. Some of the ancient mountains surrounding the city have been flattened, and the houses of the Prophet's wife Khadijah, and his close companion Abu Bakr, for example, have been demolished to make way for public lavatories and a luxury hotel.

MECCA'S INFLUENCE

Mecca is where the religion of Islam began. As such it continues to hold a powerful allure over the worldwide community of Muslims, and each year the city provides a microcosm of the Muslim world at large. More than any other site, what happens here has an effect on Muslims everywhere. Yet if the Islamic world is at a crossroads in many ways in the modern world – as many believe – this is perhaps most clearly seen in the battle between tradition and modernity played out in Islam's holiest city.

The condensed idea
Mecca remains a spiritual as well as a physical entity for all Muslims

05 Medina

The second holy city of Islam, Medina is popularly called 'city of the Prophet' (*Medina al-Nabi*) or 'the radiant city' (*al-Medina al-Munawwara*). Medina is revered as the site of the Prophet's mosque (*al-masjid an-nabawi*), the second holiest mosque in the world after Mecca's *al-masjid al-haram* (Sacred Mosque).

The Medinan mosque was originally built on a site adjacent to Muhammad's home. Today, the complex houses the Prophet's tomb, alongside those of his companions Abu Bakr and Umar ibn al-Khattab. The Prophet's tomb in Medina rivals the Kaaba in Mecca as a symbol and site of devotion for many Muslims, and visiting the tomb to offer blessings and salutations to the Prophet is a popular practice for worshippers performing their *hajj* or *umrah* pilgrimages. The prophet was buried in his wife Aisha's house and today this is part of the expanded mosque complex. The area is marked by a famous green dome rising from the mosque building.

THE MEDINAN PERIOD

Besides these sites of historical significance, Medina is considered sacred because, for over ten years, the Prophet continued to receive revelation here following his emigration from Mecca. Many see the Prophet's exodus to Medina as the fulcrum of his life. It is reported that, in 622 CE, Muhammad was invited by a delegation from the town of Yathrib (later known as Medina) to govern and to act as an arbiter because the town was suffering from internal violence and tribal conflict. So when Muhammad fled persecution in Mecca, he emigrated to Medina. He was accompanied by his Meccan followers, later referred to as 'emigrants' (*muhajirun*). The

TIMELINE

622 CE	632–656 CE
The Prophet's *hijra* to Medina, which marks the beginning of the Islamic calendar	Medina is the capital of a rapidly increasing Muslim Empire.

Medinans who welcomed Muhammad and converted to Islam are known as 'the helpers' (*ansar*). This move to Medina was the key turning point in the early history of Islam. It was in Medina that Islam first became established and that a new social and political Muslim community was born. The significance of the Prophet's move to Medina is highlighted by the fact that his companion Umar chose the *hijra* as the date for inaugurating the Islamic calendar.

In Medina, Muhammad became a ruler and judge, as well as a prophet. He was charged with governing over a religiously pluralistic society, with the town comprising Meccan emigrants, Muslim converts, pagan Arabs and also Jewish tribes. This resulted in a famous document known as the Constitution of Medina. The original copy of the text has been lost, but it is cited in numerous early Muslim sources. Under the constitution, there was to be an end to intertribal feuding. Muslim and Jewish tribes were afforded equal rights and protections under the leadership of Muhammad. Muslims today take great pride in this document and some Muslim scholars declare the Constitution of Medina to be the first written constitution in history.

The new environment of Medina, and Muhammad's position of leadership within it, is reflected in both the content and style of the Qur'anic verses. The distinction between Meccan and Medinan verses is recognizable to any reader familiar with the Qur'an. While Meccan verses typically draw on theological themes, such as the nature of God, angels and the last day, Medinan verses are often much longer and reflect on the social and political concerns of the new community. For example, Medinan verses discuss matters of marriage and divorce, inheritance and testimony in court. Muhammad's encounter with Medinan Jews and Christian tribes

> **THE PROPHET SAID, "MEDINA IS A SANCTUARY FROM THAT PLACE TO THAT. ITS TREES SHOULD NOT BE CUT AND NO HERESY SHOULD BE INNOVATED NOR ANY SIN SHOULD BE COMMITTED IN IT".**
>
> Bukhari

1924

Local ruler Ibn Saud integrates Medina and the surrounding area into the modern kingdom of Saudi Arabia.

20TH CENTURY

Medina is host to millions of Muslim pilgrims annually, who come to pay respect to the Prophet's grave during this period also sees the beginning of Qur'anic discussions on the People of the Book (*ahl al-kitab*: followers of Christianity and Judaism). Typical Medinan verses include:

> Do not marry idolatresses unless they believe; a believing woman is better than an idolatress, even if you like her. Nor shall you give your daughters in marriage to idolatrous men, unless they believe. A believing man is better than an idolater, even if you like him. (Q2:221)

> The food of those who were given the Scripture is lawful for you and your food is lawful for them. And [lawful in marriage are] chaste women from among the believers and chaste women from among those who were given the Scripture before you. (Q5:5)

During the Medinan period, the Muslim community faced a series of wars against the Meccan tribes. Alongside these battles against the Meccans, the Prophet also faced an internal threat from within Medinan society. A new group emerged during this period known as 'the hypocrites' (*al-munafiqun*). These were new converts to Islam who secretly retained their disbelief, but converted for social or political benefits or even to subvert the Muslim community from within. The Medinan passages of the Qur'an make frequent reference to this particularly dangerous threat. The hypocrites are destined for the lowest depths of hell (Q4:145) and a whole chapter – entitled The Hypocrites – is devoted to describing and condemning this group (Q63).

Medina became the final resting place for many of the closest friends and family members of the Prophet, including his daughter Fatimah, grandson Hasan, the third caliph Uthman and many other important early figures. These are buried in the famous cemetery known as *Jannat al-Baqi*. Custody of Medina transferred from the Ottoman Empire to the descendants and followers of the Saudi revivalist thinker, Muhammad ibn Abd al-Wahhab (d. 1792), in the early 20th century. Many of the large and intricate tombs that were built over the graves of these followers were destroyed. Wahhabi theology is sensitive to the visitation and veneration of graves;

it is seen as a potential compromise of monotheism as believers may erroneously worship the saintly figure or the grave itself rather than the divine. While Islamic thought, along with other monotheistic traditions, is fiercely critical of idolatry, this particular definition of idolatry is much contested across different Muslim schools.

A GOLDEN AGE

For many Muslims, the Prophet's Medina is the archetypal Islamic society. It was his time in Medina that marked the foundation of the very first Muslim community. Although for only a short period of ten years, Muhammad's leadership in Medina is commonly considered the Golden Age of Islamic history and both the creation and apogee of a true Islamic state. Mecca may have been where the revelation first occurred, but it was in Medina that the vision of a new community of believers was realized.

Jewish Medina

Judaism was well established in Medina two centuries before the Prophet's birth. While the Jews were influential, and some claim politically independent, they did not rule. They were clients of two particular Arab tribes, the Khazraj and the Aws Allah, whom they protected in return for feudal loyalty. There were many Jewish clans but the most famous are the Banu Nadir, the Banu Qaynuqa and the Banu Qurayza.

There were rabbis among the Jews of Medina to whom the Meccans went in order to ascertain the truth of Muhammad's monotheism. Muhammad arrived in Medina in 622 CE, by invitation, to arbitrate a bloody war between two of the Jewish tribes. He believed that the Jewish tribes would welcome him, but he was disappointed. At Muhammad's insistence, Medina's pagan, Muslim and Jewish clans signed a pact to protect each other. But people felt uneasy about severing old alliances and tribal agreements. The Meccans continued to weaken Muhammad's status and one incident records the killing of 700 Jews from the Banu Qurayza, who had sided with the Meccans against the Prophet. Despite episodes of conflict and peace, the Medinan Jews remained true to their faith. Theologically, they could not accept Muhammad as God's messenger, since a Messiah was to emerge from among their own people.

The condensed idea
Medinan life provided a model for Islamic society

06 The Kaaba

The Islamic world is spiritually and physically orientated towards the Kaaba, the cuboid structure located in the centre of *al-Masjid al-Haram* mosque in Mecca. It is regarded as the 'House of God' and is the holiest site for Muslims everywhere.

The Kaaba, which literally translates as 'cube' in Arabic, is clearly declared a sacred site in the Qur'an: 'Allah has made the Kaaba, the Sacred House, standing for the people' (Q5:97). Elsewhere, Qur'anic references to God's 'sacred house' or the 'first house' of worship are invariably taken by commentators as implicit references to the Kaaba in Mecca. It is also believed that the Kaaba is but an earthly symbol of the celestial *Bayt al-Ma'mur*; a divine replica located directly above in the heavens and mentioned in the Qur'an (Q52:4). This is the site where, according to *hadith* traditions, the angels perform their prayers and worship God.

THE ORIGINS OF THE KAABA

The story of the Kaaba is central to an understanding of Islamic history and prophecy. It is said that the original structure was erected during the time of Adam and Eve, and that it marked the first shrine dedicated solely to the worship of the one God. Destroyed during the floods of Noah, it was rebuilt by the prophet Abraham and his son, Ishmael. This is alluded to in various parts in the Qur'an, which speak of Abraham and his son building a 'house' for the worship of God (Q2:127). Islamic tradition recounts how, in the centuries after Abraham, the pre-Islamic Arabs lapsed into idolatry and the Kaaba consequently became a shrine for many idols worshipped by

TIMELINE

570 CE	**623 CE**
Pre-Islamic story that God stopped a man named Abraha destroying the Kaaba.	Muhammad switches the direction of prayer (*qibla*), from Jerusalem towards the Kaaba

various Arabian tribes. This continued until, in one of the most famous episodes of the life story of the Prophet, Muhammad is reported to have smashed the idols in the Kaaba upon his successful conquest of Mecca in 632 CE. The early biographer Ibn Ishaq records the event:

> GOD IS THE LIGHT OF THE HEAVENS AND THE EARTH.
> Q24:35

> The apostle went to the Kaaba and rode seven times around it on his camel . . . it was (then) opened to him, and he entered. There he found a pigeon made of aloe-wood, and he broke this idol with his own hand and threw it outside. The other idols stood fixed with lead, and the prophet made a sign with his stick in the direction of the idols, saying 'truth has arrived and falsehood has gone, because falsehood was perishable.' (Q17:33) Nor, did he point to the front of any idol, but it fell down on its back, nor did he point to its back, but it fell down on its face. Not one idol remained standing . . . (He shouted) 'People of Quraysh! Allah has freed from you from the arrogance of idolatry!'

The Prophet thus famously cleansed the Kaaba of idols and returned it to an original state of monotheistic worship, as initially established by Abraham. The Kaaba therefore stands as both a witness to key events during the Prophet's lifetime, and also harkens much further back to Islam's spiritual origins with Abraham.

THE APPEARANCE OF THE KAABA

The Kaaba is not worshipped in itself. Muslims do not worship the walls or the structure of the Kaaba. Rather, the Kaaba is symbolically significant, for it provides the ritual space in which one directs one's worship towards God. All prayer is directed towards the Kaaba and this is known as the *qibla*. Also of note is the unusual appearance of the Kaaba. In many ways this is a most unique religious icon. It is not an elaborate, grandiose or lavishly

630 CE	**692** CE	**2016**
Muslim conquest of Mecca. Muhammad destroys the idols	Kaaba bombarded with stones in the second siege of Mecca	Kaaba receives millions of visitors annually

Dressing the Kaaba

The black cloth that drapes the Kaaba is called the *kiswah*. It is draped annually on the ninth day during the month of *hajj* and every year the old *kiswah* is removed, cut into small pieces and divided among individuals ranging from ordinary people to foreign dignitaries.

Most Western studies of the *kiswah* have not attempted to explain why it is hung on the Kaaba. Some have suggested that Muslims draped the Kaaba with black cloth in order symbolically to claim that God still dwelled in a tent, a belief supposedly rooted in the Arabs' bedouin past. Muhammad and the Muslims in Mecca did not actually drape the Kaaba until the conquest of the city in 630 CE, just two years before the Prophet died. This practice was continued by the caliphs, who varied the number of times they draped the Kaaba each year.

It has been argued that the materials out of which the *kiswah* were made also had strong feminine connotations. Gold thread, silk and satin were seldom used in men's clothing because these materials were considered inappropriate for male dress. However, according to the Qur'an, the clothing worn in paradise by both men and women will be made of silk, gold and pearls. God will admit those who believe into gardens where 'They shall be adorned therein with bracelets of gold and their garments there will be of fine silk and brocade, reclining therein on adorned couches' (Q18:31).

decorated structure, but rather the exact opposite: a simple cuboid, draped in black with gold Qur'anic inscriptions. The Kaaba is characterized by its simplicity and has an almost otherworldly appearance.

THE BLACK STONE

Located in the eastern corner is the Black Stone, commonly believed to be an ancient meteorite. Muslim tradition reveres the black stone as an ancient Islamic relic that was sent down from heaven to instruct Adam and Eve as a guide to build the original Kaaba. To this day, as pilgrims circle the Kaaba during the *hajj* pilgrimage, many try to stop and kiss the Black Stone, emulating the practice of Muhammad. Throughout the course of Muslim history the Kaaba has had to be rebuilt several times, on account of either natural disasters or owing to damage inflicted during times of conflict. Muslims believe the only piece remaining from the original structure is the Black Stone.

THE SIGNIFICANCE OF THE KAABA
The Kaaba remains the enduring symbol of Islam. It is this site at which the sacred and the profane meet. The Kaaba also provides a tangible link connecting the Muslim present with its past. It is also through the Kaaba – more so than any other symbol or image – that a diverse, global Muslim community is reminded of its shared heritage and bonds.

Thousands of Muslims circumambulate the Kaaba every day; millions of Muslim homes and prayer mats are adorned with images of the Kaaba; and over one billion Muslims turn towards the Kaaba as part of their daily prayers. Every mosque in the world faces the direction of the Kaaba.

The *hajj* pilgrimage, one of the central pillars of Muslim religious life, is significant precisely owing to the Qur'anic command for Muslims to visit the Kaaba in person at least once in a lifetime. This is obligatory for all Muslims who are financially and physically able. The rituals of the *hajj* take Muslims to various places, but the most dramatic image of the *hajj* each year is that of hundreds of thousands of Muslims circumambulating the Kaaba in silent and vocal prayer.

The condensed idea
There is someone circling the Kaaba every minute, every day

07 Sunni Islam

Sunni Islam is the biggest denomination of Muslims in the world, constituting 85–90 per cent of the Muslim population, globally. There was no movement that promoted Sunni Islam but this branch of Islam emerged as the mainstream body of Muslims, both politically and doctrinally.

Sunni Islam is sometimes referred to as 'orthodox Islam', but this does not mean that there was a unified way of being Sunni before the various divisions in the Islamic world. It is normative by being the largest denomination, but both Sunni and Shi`a Islam underwent centuries of competing ideologies and divisions before they settled on their respective identities and bodies of knowledge.

SUNNI ORIGINS

The word 'Sunni' comes from the term *sunna*, which originally referred to the established customs of previous generations, caliphs or areas, but eventually came to refer to the exemplary conduct of the Prophet. The actions and sayings of Muhammad were deemed worthy of emulation and ultimately became a source of authority for Muslim societies.

The fundamental starting point that came to distinguish Sunni Islam from Shi`a Islam is that Muhammad's close companions elected Abu Bakr, rather than Ali ibn Abi Talib (Ali), as the rightful caliph after Muhammad's death. This first caliphate established its role as one that upheld religious law as well as exercising political rule. Sunnism

TIMELINE

632 CE	661–750 CE	750–1258
Abu Bakr chosen as first leader of the Muslim community	Umayyad Caliphate is the first great dynasty to rule the Muslim Empire	Abbasid Caliphate makes Baghdad capital of the Muslim Empire

identified itself on the basis of such Prophetic sayings as, those who follow the *sunna* and the agreement of the community would achieve salvation, and that the *sunna* was what the Prophet and his companions practised. In many ways Sunnis hold a centrist position – one between the messianic teachings of Shi`a Islam and the violent puritanism of the Kharijites (the first-known Islamic sect).

> **GUIDANCE IS NOT ATTAINED EXCEPT WITH KNOWLEDGE, AND CORRECT DIRECTION IS NOT ATTAINED EXCEPT WITH PATIENCE.**
>
> Ibn Taymiyyah (1263–1328)

In Islam, orthodoxy is not only that which earns a broad concensus from the community, but also that which avoids extremes. It tries to carve out a middle way based on historical precedent of the companions and is preserved by pious scholars. As Daniel Brown said in *A New Introduction to Islam*, 'To be Sunni was to be neither a qadarite advocate of free will, nor a jabarite determinist, neither a Kharijite nor Murji'ite, neither a stripper of God's attributes nor an anthropomorphist.' These ideologies and schools did not represent true Islam.

The political theology of Sunnism has been centred on the sovereignty of law, but also on a diffuse relationship between political leaders, religious leaders and the public. Sunni orthodoxy began to be articulated during the Abbasid period with its particular understanding of *sunna*. This comprised of loyalty to the six books of *hadith*, including the famous collections of *Sahih al-Bukhari* and *Sahih Muslim*. Theological belief was encapsulated in six articles of faith, namely: the reality of the one true God; belief in God's angels; belief in previously revealed scriptures, including the Torah and the Gospels; belief in previous prophets; belief in the Day of Judgement; and belief in predestination – that God's will remains supreme. The principles and legal output of the four main Sunni legal schools became central to maintaining a certain type of orthodoxy and orthopraxy, despite cultural and regional differences across the Islamic world.

10TH CENTURY	1924	1990s–2016
Al-Ash`ari (d. 935) develops a theology that comes to define Sunni Islam	Ottoman Caliphate, the last caliphate of Sunni Islam, disbanded by Mustafa Kemal Ataturk	Sunni Islam increasingly linked with jihadist violence, through groups, such as the Taliban, Al Qaeda and Islamic State

Ibn Taymiyyah – Sheikh al-Islam

The decline of Abbasid rule came with invasions from the east by the powerful Mongol armies and from the west, with the Crusader forces that captured Palestine and parts of Syria. One response to this trauma among medieval Sunni thinkers was to look back nostalgically to notions of a glorious Islamic past, while condemning the present state of Muslim societies.

Ibn Taymiyyah (1263–1328) is considered one of the greatest revivalist thinkers of this period. A follower of the Hanbali school of law, he remains a controversial thinker. He is known for his untiring polemics against perceived innovations and heresies in Islam, his frequent imprisonment, and famous legal rulings (*fatawa*), which included preaching military jihad against the (converted Muslim) Mongol rulers. He argued for each generation to return directly to the original sources of the Qur'an and Prophetic *sunna*.

Central to Ibn Taymiyyah's approach was his locating of interpretive authority in the first three generations of Muslims – the companions of the Prophet, the successors and the children of the successors. These generations were closest to the original divine source and thus, for Ibn Taymiyyah, they understood the religion better than all later generations. His message was therefore clear: the closer one is to the Prophet and his companions, the closer one is to divine truth.

This kind of revivalism is a recurring event in Sunni Islam with notable thinkers in each generation responding to the political and social misfortunes of their time. Critical self-evaluation, combined with preaching a reformed Islam inspired by the Prophetic years, is an ongoing aspect of Sunni political thought.

SUNNI THEOLOGIANS

While there are many great names associated with Sunni Islam, the greatest is probably Abu al-Hasan al-Ash`ari (873–935) who had been a promising Mu`tazilite theologian, but who gave this up to study traditionalist *hadith*. His most famous doctrines are theological in nature. On the issue of free will and predestination, for example, he stated that God preordained human acts but that humans acquire responsibility for them (*kasb*) before they are performed in real time.

On the issue of anthropomorphic references to God in the Qur'an, such as God's hands or God's face, Ibn Hanbal (720–855), another giant of Islamic theology, had argued that these were to be taken literally 'without asking how' (*bila kayfa*). He resisted the Mu`tazilite doctrine of the time, which interpreted these verses metaphorically, and for this he was imprisoned and tortured. Al-Ash`ari also opposed the metaphorical interpretation, but argued against any similarity between God and his creation. He followed Ibn Hanbal with the doctrine of *bila kayfa*. Humankind cannot know how God has eyes, hearing and so on; these facts must simply be accepted. Al-Ash`ari also wrote a creed that came to sum up the dogmatic basis of Sunni Islam.

SUNNI ISLAM IN MODERN TIMES

Sunni Islam remains the dominant face of the religion and is largely united, despite the absence of any centralized authority or legal framework. Today, Sunni Islam captures the headlines for a range of political reasons. It often emerges as a voice in opposition, whether it be in opposition to movements such as Wahhabism and Salafism.

It is tragic that Sunni Islam's biggest battle is with militant groups, such as Islamic State, who see their triumphs as a triumph of Sunni Islam against Shi`ism and other minority groups. They see their combative jihad as restoring a pristine Muslim state, but for most Muslims observing the brutal actions of Islamic State, nothing could be further from the truth.

The condensed idea
Religious authority resides in scripture and the community

08 Shi`a Islam

Shi`ism is one of two main denominational divisions among Muslims, the other being Sunnism (see Chapter 7). Those adhering to Shi`ism are referred to as Shi`i as well as the collective noun Shi`a. While the term 'Sunni-Shi`i schism' is often used to discuss the political and religious separation, the Shi`a are much smaller in number than the Sunnis with Shi`a Muslims comprising 10 to 15 per cent of the global Muslim population.

Shi`a-majority countries include Iran, Iraq, Azerbaijan and Bahrain, with significant minorities found throughout the Middle East and in countries like Nigeria and Pakistan. The origins of Shi`a Islam stem from political differences in the early Muslim community. Theological differences did not develop until after this political split. The major issue confronting the early Muslim community after the death of the Prophet in 632 CE was a dispute over leadership. One group of followers gathered around Ali, the Prophet's cousin and son-in-law. This group was to become the Shi`a, a contraction of the Arabic term *Shi`at Ali*, or 'partisans of Ali'.

SHI`I PIETY

Shi`a Muslims believe Muhammad explicitly elected Ali as his chosen successor during his lifetime, at a place called Ghadir Khumm. Many such claims are found in *hadith* narrations found in both Sunni and Shi`a collections. In one famous *hadith*, the Prophet is said to have likened their relationship to the prophets Moses and Aaron. In another, Muhammad is quoted as saying: 'To whomsoever I am *mawla* (guardian/

TIMELINE

656 CE	680 CE	941 CE
Ali becomes caliph	Martyrdom of Husayn at Karbala	Beginning of 'Greater Occultation'

trustee), Ali is his *mawla'*. Shi`a thought has interpreted these as clearly asserting the Prophet's choice of Ali as leader, whereas Sunni Muslims read the same traditions simply as an expression of the especially close bond between the Prophet and his cousin and son-in-law, Ali.

Arguably, the definitive break between Sunni and Shi`a Islam occurred in the year 680 CE, during the Battle of Karbala, in modern-day Iraq. In this battle, Husayn – Ali's son and the Prophet's grandson – fought the ruling Sunni caliph for leadership of the Muslim community. Husayn's forces were massively outnumbered, and he was killed and beheaded. All Muslims consider the murder of the Prophet's grandson a tragedy, but for the Shi`a, Husayn's death plays a distinct role in their religious consciousness. The events of Karbala have become the defining feature of Shi`i piety. Shi`a Muslims see Husayn's actions as a call for justice, and the tragedy of Karbala plays a central role in the development of Shi`i theology. Today, the Battle of Karbala is commemorated on the Day of Ashura, the tenth day of Muharram, the first month of the Muslim calendar. This is a day of remembrance and mourning for Shi`a Muslims, often accompanied by highly evocative passion plays. Popular practices on this day can include self-flagellation, seeking to emulate the suffering of Husayn. The phrase, 'every day is Ashura and every land is Karbala' has become a popular motif in Shi`i thought and piety.

> **LIVE AMONG PEOPLE IN SUCH A MANNER THAT IF YOU DIE THEY WEEP OVER YOU AND IF YOU ARE ALIVE THEY CRAVE FOR YOUR COMPANY.**
>
> Imam Ali,
> *Nahjul Balagha*

THE SHI`A IMAM

While Sunni Muslims see religious authority residing in the community of believers, as with the election of the Prophet's companion Abu Bakr as his successor, Shi`a Muslims locate religious authority in the Prophet's family. Ali is considered the first 'imam', or leader of the community, the position then extending to his family and descendants. For Shi`a Muslims,

1500	1925	1979
Twelver Shi`ism becomes main religion	End of Qajar dynasty; Reza Khan becomes Iran's first shah of the Pahlavi dynasty	Shi`a revolution in Iran and establishment of Islamic Republic under Khomeini

New sectarian conflicts

Violence between Islam's sects has been rare historically, with most of the deadly sectarian attacks directed by clerics or political leaders, rather than arising from within communities. Extremist groups are the chief actors in sectarian killings today. Syria's civil war, in which one-quarter of a million people have been killed and 11 million displaced, has amplified sectarian tensions. The war began with peaceful protests in 2011 calling for an end to the Assad regime and its repression of Syria's majority Sunni population. Tens of thousands of Syrian Sunnis joined rebel groups, such as Ahrar al-Sham, the Islamic Front and al-Qaeda's Al-Nusra Front, all of which employ anti-Shi`a rhetoric; similar numbers of Syrian Shi`as and Alawis enlisted with an Iran-backed militia known as the National Defense Force to fight for the Assad regime. Sunni extremist recruitment is rising and Shi`a militant groups are also gaining strength, in part to confront the threat of Sunni extremism. In 2015, the Islamic State claimed responsibility for, among other attacks, bombing Shi`a worshippers in Kuwait; attacking Sunni and Shi`a mosques in Saudi Arabia and carrying out suicide bombings in a Shi`a-majority district of south Beirut. These growing sectarian clashes have created a revival of transnational jihadi networks, whose use of social media to recruit young people to their causes, poses a global threat.

these imams are inheritors of the Prophet's bloodline and possess special qualities. They are considered infallible: incapable of sin, in receipt of esoteric knowledge and alone possess the keys to interpreting divine sources and their secret meanings. In Shi`ism, *hadith* traditions need not be traced back to the Prophet himself; the imams' infallibility means they become an equally authoritative point of reference.

Internal schisms within Shi`a Islam emerged from different understandings of the leadership of imams – namely, how many there had been, and when the line of imams came to an end. The dominant Shi`a school, known as the 'Twelver' school (*Ithna 'Ashariyya*), believes in a line of twelve imams, which ended when the twelfth imam, the Imam al-Mahdi, entered a period of 'occultation', or disappearance from the world. It is believed the Mahdi will return to establish justice and true Islamic law before the Day of Judgement. Before this time, Shi`a religious clerics, known as *ayatollah* (literally, 'sign of God'), are tasked with leading the community of believers.

Other Shi`a subgroups, such as the Zaydi school (or 'Fivers'), concentrated mostly in Yemen, believe the line of imams stopped after the death of the fifth imam, Zayd ibn Ali (d. 730 CE). Zaydis also reject the concept of occultation. Another offshoot of Shi`a thought, the Ismaili school led today by the Aga Khan, is sometimes called 'Seveners' as its adherents believe in a line of seven imams, culminating in Muhammad ibn Ismail in 740 CE.

SUNNI AND SHI`A DIFFERENCES

The status of the imam is one of several clear theological differences between the Sunni and Shi`a schools. Perhaps the most controversial issue, however, relates to Shi`a views of the first three leaders of the Muslim community, Abu Bakr, Umar and Uthman. Sunni Muslims revere these figures as pious companions of the Prophet and as 'Rightly Guided Caliphs', whereas Shi`a tradition sees their rule as illegitimate and impediments to Ali's rightful leadership. Some features unique to Shi`a Islam include the practice of temporary marriage (*nikah al-muta*) and the concept of *taqiyyah* – a legal dispensation allowing a person to deny his faith or commit otherwise blasphemous acts if living under threat of persecution. The latter reflects the minority position the Shi`a have often endured under Sunni rule and the history of Sunni persecution against the imams, most of whom were killed by Sunni rulers. Today, both temporary marriage and *taqiyyah* have become common features of Sunni, anti-Shi`a sectarian polemic. Yet civil conflict in many parts of the Muslim world has also seen cooperation between the two sects.

The condensed idea
The imam's authority is both religious and political

09 Caliphate

Ever since the death of the Prophet, the title *khalifa* has been adopted by the head of the Muslim state. Occurring twice in the Qur'an in its singular form the word, meaning successor or representative, is used in multiple ways, but most notably to mean a successor to the 'messenger of God' or the 'vicegerent of God.'

The traditional Sunni Muslim account is that, after the death of the Prophet, his friend and father-in-law Abu Bakr was elected the first caliph (*khalifa*). The standard Arabian practice at the time was for the prominent men of a tribe to consult amongst themselves and elect a capable leader from within the group. This process became known as a *shura* and some describe the process as bearing the marks of a rudimentary democracy.

THE RIGHTLY GUIDED

The wars of expansion began under Abu Bakr, and when he died in 634 CE, his successor Umar laid the foundations of a political society. On Umar's death in 644 CE, Uthman took over as the third caliph. By this time, the former Sasanian and Byzantine territories had all come under Arab Muslim rule. Under Uthman some of the Mediterranean islands, including Cyprus and Crete, also came under Muslim rule.

When Uthman was assassinated in 656 CE, Ali, the cousin and son-in-law of the Prophet, became the fourth caliph. His supporters claimed that he had been passed over three times, even though he was the rightful heir

TIMELINE

632 CE	661 CE	661–750 CE
Election of Abu Bakr as the first caliph following Muhammad's death	Period of the 'rightly guided caliphs' comes to an end with the assassination of Ali	Umayyad Caliphate established, with its capital in Damascus

to the Prophet. But he also faced opposition from rebel armies, which included the Prophet's youngest wife Aisha. While Ali emerged victorious from the famous Battle of the Camel, he was assassinated in 661 CE and the period came to an end.

The first four caliphs were known as the *Rashidun* or 'the rightly guided'. They exercised enormous political control and witnessed the rapid expansion of Islam. Yet while the Sunni caliph was the leader of the Muslim community, with responsibilities that included upholding the faith and the law, the legislative power of the caliph – and subsequently the sultan – was restricted by the scholarly elite, the *ulema*. It is argued that the early caliphs saw their authority as coming straight from God, and that meant obedience by the populace to their rule.

> **WHAT MADE AL QAEDA RETRIEVE THE DOCTRINE OF MILITANT JIHAD, AND BREIVIK THE IDEAS OF CRUSADE AND RECONQUEST, IS A SENSE OF SIEGE. SO, WE SHOULD HELP BOTH WESTERNERS AND MUSLIMS GET RID OF THAT SENSE BY EASING THEIR POLITICAL TENSIONS AND BY FOSTERING DIALOGUE BETWEEN THEM.**
>
> Mustafa Akyol

The subsequent ruling dynasties and empires, such as the Umayyad and the Abbasids, ruled over expansive empires and diverse cultures with Damascus and Baghdad as glittering capitals. All this came to an end with the Mongol invasion of Baghdad in 1258. After this period, the caliph was more of a religious figurehead with little power. The last Sunni caliphate was the Ottoman caliphate, a rule that had been claimed by the Turkish sultans since the 14th century. It was abolished in 1924 under Kemal Ataturk's secular reforms.

GOD'S DEPUTY

While political and religious rule remains closely tied to the concept of caliphate, the Qur'anic reference to *khalifa* occurs in one particular sense in the creation story, 'Behold,' your Lord said to the angels, 'I will create a vicegerent (*khalifa*) on Earth.' Exactly

750–1258	1258	1924	2014
Abbasid Caliphate establishes its capital in Baghdad	Mongol invasion of Baghdad marks end of Abbasid Caliphate	Ottoman Caliphate, the last Sunni Caliphate, is abolished by Kemal Ataturk	Islamic State leader, Abu Bakr al-Baghdadi, announces return of the caliphate for all Muslims

The appeal of the caliphate

In June 2014, the jihadists of Islamic State revived their identity with a hashtag, #CaliphateRestored. They also attempted to erase what they saw as artificial colonial borders, with other memorable hashtags such as #SykesPicotOver.

This rebranding began at the start of the holy month of Ramadan in which the jihadists declared, 'We clarify to the Muslims that with this declaration of *khalifah* (caliphate), it is incumbent upon all Muslims to pledge allegiance to the Khalifa Ibrahim and support him'. The self-proclaimed caliph Ibrahim uses the name Abu Bakr al-Baghdadi – a reference to the first caliph of 632 CE.

The message that Islamic State continually promotes is that the Muslim world is in decline because there is no caliphate, that the Muslim world has become too Westernized, and that its own particular caliphate system will restore Islam to its former glory and power. This kind of rhetoric appeals to many who are looking for a cause.

Islamic State is not the first group to call for a caliphate since the Ottoman caliphate was abolished in 1924. In modern times, Hizb ut-Tahrir (Party of Liberation) and al-Qaeda have campaigned unsuccessfully for its restoration. Hizb ut-Tahrir was established in 1953 as a Sunni Muslim organization in Jerusalem and has spread to more than 50 countries. Its ideological raison d'etre is to establish a caliphate that is transnational and it encourages Muslims to have loyalty to religion above loyalty to the nation state. While very active in the West, it is banned in some countries.

what is meant by *khalifa* in this context is open to interpretation, and can be compared, to some extent, to the biblical *Imago Dei*, 'man made in the image of God' (Genesis 1:26-27). However, *khalifa* does imply some kind of successor or deputy who will settle on Earth. Early Muslim commentary also suggested that Adam – that is, the generic concept of man – may be God's representative in 'exercising judgement with justice' (Q38:26). The Qur'an advises Adam and the sons of Adam that the status of *khalifa* means that they are being entrusted to look after the Earth, the implication being that the Earth and its riches are in man's care (*amana*):

It is we who have placed you with authority on Earth and provided you therein with means for the fulfilment of your life. (Q7:10)

Verses such as 'We created man in the best of forms' (Q95:4) and 'He fashioned you in the best of images (Q40:64) indicate multiple perspectives about man, his place in creation and his relationship with God.

THE CALIPH CONCEPT TODAY

For many Muslims, the caliphate still appeals as a unifying power. In the post-colonial period, pan-Arab nationalists after the Second World War all went for a secular version of a caliphate. Gamal Abdel Nasser proclaimed a union of Egypt and Syria, in which he aimed to add Iraq. In more recent times the concept has appealed to those Muslims who imagine the Muslim *ummah* united under this position, a leader who, with God's blessing, dispenses law and justice throughout the countries of Islam. It is not surprising, therefore, that the concept of *khalifa* is invoked by various zealots, including militant or jihadist groups who invoke the *khalifa* as a way of rallying Muslims together against the West.

The most extreme example of such a group is the brutal Islamic State. What most sets it apart is the group's claim to have restored the Islamic caliphate, thus eradicating decades of supposed humiliation by outsiders and those Arab rulers who became incompetent as Muslim power declined. The status of victimhood and the desire for revenge is a potent mix. The Islamic State leader Abu Bakr al-Baghdadi, sees his state as the Islamic utopia with his messianic call, 'Rush O Muslims to your state'. It may sound absurd to many that they actually have a state, but their brutal and violent regime has become one of the biggest threats to global peace in the modern world.

The condensed idea
There is no Islamic caliphate

10 Witness to faith

The Muslim witness to faith is contained in the words, 'I declare that there is no god but God and Muhammad is the messenger of God.' This *shahada* is the verbal recognition of the reality of God and the prophecy of Muhammad. Declaring these words is the central, foundational act upon which all Islamic practice depends.

The *shahada* literally means to 'bear witness' or to 'testify'. The first half of the creed defines Islamic monotheism. This is the cosmic truth of the oneness of God, the belief that he alone is worthy of worship. The second part of the *shahada* is more specific and recognizes the means by which God gives guidance to mankind. All fundamental doctrines in Islam derive from the *shahada*, including the authority of the Qur'an, belief in angels, the long line of prophets preceding Muhammad and the Day of Judgement. Indeed, it is possible to view the entirety of Muslim theology and law as an explanation of the *shahada*. Shi`a Muslims extend the *shahada* to include a third line: 'and Ali is the friend of God' (*wa' aliyyun waliyyullah*).

> **SAY: HE IS ALLAH, THE ONE AND ONLY! ALLAH, THE ETERNAL, ABSOLUTE; HE BEGETTETH NOT NOR IS HE BEGOTTEN. AND THERE IS NONE LIKE UNTO HIM.**
>
> Q112:1–4

THE PRACTICE OF SHAHADA

The full *shahada* itself is absent in the Qur'an, although there are separate references to 'no God but God' (Q37:35, Q47:19) and 'Muhammad is the messenger of God'. (Q48:29) Neither is there any indication of the precise ritual act that Muslims later made of it, as the first of the 'five pillars' – those five duties or practices that a Muslim must perform as part of daily life (see page 88).

TIMELINE

610 CE	7TH CENTURY
Muhammad receives first revelation	Rapid spread of Islam

In one verse, the Qur'an calls those declaring the first half of the creed as 'those of knowledge', alongside God and the angels:

> Allah witnesses that there is no god except him, and [so do] the angels and those of knowledge – [that he is] maintaining [creation] in justice. There is no deity except him, the exalted in might, the wise. (Q3:18)

Jews and Christians similarly declare that there is no God but God. In many ways it is Jewish and Christian agreement with the first half of the *shahada*, yet rejection of the second part of the *shahada* that confirms Muhammad's prophecy and explains the Qur'an's ambivalence towards what it refers to as the People of the Book (Jews and Christians).

A SACRED RITUAL

Converting to Islam requires no more than an open declaration of the *shahada*. It is recommended, though not generally considered obligatory, that this be in the presence of two witnesses. Central to this act of conversion, however, is the individual's sincere intention and their understanding of the importance of the words.

This marks the *shahada* as a sacred ritual. For this reason, simply declaring the words without sincerely meaning them – such as a non-Muslim

Conversion to Islam

Over the last few decades, most social scientists, and indeed many theologians, have been predicting the complete secularization of society because institutional religion is on the decline. In the UK during the 20th century, weekly church-going numbers declined to less than 15 per cent, and more than half of those who attend church at the age of 13 will have ceased to do so by the time they reach 20. Despite this formal decline within Western Christianity, conversion to Islam is growing in Europe and converts have all kinds of social, moral and personal reasons for reciting the *shahada* as the first step to becoming a Muslim.

LATE 7TH CENTURY	21ST CENTURY
Shahada first appears as inscriptions on coins and on facades of buildings	*Shahada* appears on black standard of jihadist groups

The one God debate

Muslims and Christians recognize one another as believing in one God. But how they see this 'oneness' can vary. Historically, this issue exercised the minds of both Christian and Muslim philosophers and theologians. In the 20th century, the famous Swiss reformed theologian Karl Barth (1886–1968) criticized Islam for its 'noisy fanaticism regarding the one God'. For Barth, Islam emphasized the oneness of God in all its creeds whereas Christianity emphasized the uniqueness of God. He found Islamic monotheism no different than paganism. Muslims on the other hand were challenged by Christian monotheism in the doctrines of the Incarnation of Christ and the Holy Trinity.

teacher in a classroom, for example – would not make one a Muslim. While sincerely expressing these words is all that is formally required to become a Muslim, most Muslims agree that faith is not genuine or sincere if the *shahada* is not followed by other practices, such as prayers or fasting. In other words, one's Islam should not remain simply verbal, but should be followed with practical conduct. While declaring the *shahada* is therefore the first pillar of the faith, it is anticipated that the Muslim will live according to the principles of the *shahada*, as expressed in the other four pillars (that is, through prayer, almsgiving, making a pilgrimage and fasting through Ramadan).

RECITING THE SHAHADA

In daily life, Muslims frequently recite the *shahada* as a central part of religious practice. Examples of such practice include a father whispering the words into the ear of a newborn child, and someone whispering them into the ear of a dying person. The five canonical prayers also include a silent recitation of the *shahada*, with the believer resting on their knees after prostration. The call to prayer (*adhan*) similarly includes two recitations of the creed. It is therefore a statement that runs throughout the daily life of the believer. Particularly in Sufi circles, the *shahada* can be repeated hundreds of times as part of Sufi contemplative prayer.

VISUAL REPRESENTATIONS

Rarely has a statement been the source of as much artistic inspiration within Islam as the *shahada*. Its only rivals, perhaps, are specific Qur'anic verses such as the first chapter, entitled Opening (*al-fatiha*). It is common to see calligraphic designs of the *shahada* within mosques, decorating Muslim homes and even as car stickers. The creed is also imprinted on the flags of several Muslim countries, such as Saudi Arabia and Somaliland.

In recent years, the *shahada* has also been used on the banners of violent jihadi movements such as Islamic State. The Arabic lettering, with the text of the *shahada* cast in white against a plain black background, has become a symbol readily identifiable with terrorist groups. For them, the first creed of Islam is now a cry of war.

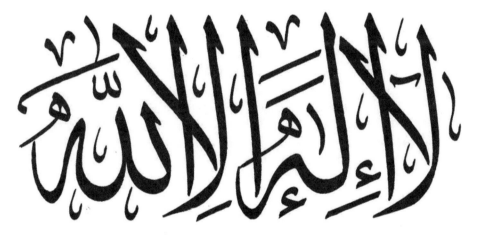

The condensed idea
Statements of faith take centuries to formulate

11 Creation

In Islam, God is the creator of the seen and unseen worlds. The Qur'an gives various accounts of creation, but the most significant story is the creation of Adam. This event is not a quiet affair, but rather announced to the angels as a turning point in the destiny of the Earth itself. The reasons for creating humanity remain with God, however; they are not disclosed.

Stories of creation feature frequently in the Qur'an, always pointing to a purpose that many do not understand or know. The Qur'an says, 'We have not created the heavens and the Earth and all that is in them as a game; we have created them for no other purpose but the truth, but most people do not know this' (Q44:38-39). The earth, sea, atmosphere and all the creatures that they contain are not the result of some divine sport, nor are they the casual result of processes begun and left to follow their own destiny by an irresponsible creator. The approach of the Qur'an to Nature is that Nature is a blessing, it provides a spiritual context that demands that we always think beyond the temporal until the Day of Judgement. We cannot ignore Nature's signs because they direct us always to God.

GOD'S CALIPH

Human creation sets the context for humankind's purpose and position: Man is to be God's representative on this Earth, God's *khalifa*. This relationship between humankind and God is therefore marked from the very beginning as a relationship with a moral purpose. Man's relative lowly nature – his physical essence is clay (*tin*) – contrasts with the lofty

TIMELINE

6TH CENTURY BCE	c. 408–318 BCE
First draft of Pentateuch (Torah) emerges	Writing of the Dead Sea Scrolls, many of which contain fragments of Hebrew scripture, including Genesis

status God bestows on him as one predetermined to have knowledge and it is this knowledge that designates him a place at the centre of creation. God distinguishes human beings from other beings by breathing into Adam of his own spirit; thus, humanity comes into the fullness of its being only through that final breath – that is, the element of divine origin in the human make-up.

The Qur'an advises Adam and the sons of Adam that the status of *khalifa* means that they are being entrusted to look after the Earth and that the bounties of the heavens and the Earth are in man's care (*amana*):

> It is we who have placed you with authority on Earth and provided you therein with means for the fulfilment of your life. (Q7:10)

Man is both part of nature and yet above nature, and his voluntary stewardship means that he is responsible for the well-being of nature.

RISING TO THE CHALLENGE

Central to any understanding of man's relationship to God and man's relationship to nature is a curious Qur'anic verse: 'Look, We offered the *trust* to the heavens and the Earth and the mountains, but they refused to carry it and were afraid of it. But man accepted [the challenge]. He has indeed been unjust and ignorant.' (Q33:72) It is as if God himself is bemused at man's temerity that he can be faithful to this momentous

DO THOSE WHO DISBELIEVE NOT SEE THAT THE HEAVENS (SKIES) AND THE EARTH WERE JOINED TOGETHER AND WE RIPPED THEM APART?

Q21:20

A 17th-century Mughal illustration celebrating mythical and real creatures from the 'Island of Zanj' (modern southeast Africa).

651/652 CE

Uthmanic codex

1930

Muhammad Iqbal explores Qur'anic creation story

Best of form

The Qur'an says that human beings are created in the 'best of form' (Q95:4), but not in God's image. However, one ambiguous Prophetic *hadith* refers to man being created in God's image or form: 'God created Adam according to his form'.

The variances on this *hadith* are based on a little-known story that the Prophet once passed a man who was beating his servant on the face and said to him, 'Do not beat his face for God created Adam in his form'. The use of the word 'form' here was both accepted and contested by theologians and philosophers. Among them, the Sufi al-Hallaj (d. 922) declared that there was no radical antinomy between Creator and the created man.

When the angels were ordered to prostrate themselves before Adam, it was as a divine form. The famous theologian al-Ghazali (d. 1111) was aware that there were difficulties with ascribing Adam's form to God's form. For the theologians, anthropomorphic terms in the Qur'an posed a dilemma. How could God be characterized in terms such as 'living', 'seeing' or 'hearing' and yet these attributes remain distinct from the way humankind lives and hears and sees? Many found a compromise in ascribing corporeality to an invisible God, namely, that any likeness in form between man and God did not mean any likeness in attributes – the comparison is figuratively only.

promise of looking after God's creation, especially when all else declined this invitation. A day will come when we will all have to give an account of our stewardship over the natural world. In a powerfully poetic, even haunting, passage the Qur'an invokes this day and presents the image of the natural universe rising up to accuse humankind of its crimes:

On that day, [the Earth] will tell its stories, because your Lord will inspire it. On that day, humankind will come forth in small groups to show its deeds. Whoever has committed even a gram of goodness will see it then, and whoever has done even a gram of evil will see it at that time. (Q99: 4–8)

The Qur'an does not say that human beings are created in God's image, even if they are created in the best of form. The divine breath is an essential element in the completion of humankind, but it does not explain how, or whether, this makes humanity godlike in any way.

THE WORLD'S DEPENDENCE ON GOD

While the story of Adam's creation is the most powerful event in the God–man narrative, Muslim philosophers and theologians reflect on how creation and God exist together. Some of the philosophers portray creation as an eternal emanation from God. For others, God's eternal will chose when the world originated. The crux of the debate was whether God creates the world eternally out of the perfection of his nature or out of nothing according to his free will? For the philosophers and theologians, the Qur'an offers different understandings of viewing the world's dependence on God.

God creates out of love

A fundamental question for early Muslims was: why did God create? There is a famous *hadith qudsi*, 'I was a hidden treasure then I desired to be known, so I created a creation to which I made myself known; then they knew me.' The very purpose of creation is for God to reveal himself. For Ṣufis such as Ibn al-`Arabi and al-Hallaj, this is not because God needs creation in any way to realize his fullness, but because God's creative love is so strong that it triggers the whole process of creation. God does not become less God or more God in the act of creation, but something within God inspires a movement of creative freedom.

For Ibn al-`Arabi, love becomes a universal principle encompassing the actions of all creation – that is, the basis by which all phenomena are explicable. It is the movement of love that creates the existence of the world. According to Ibn al-`Arabi's cosmogony, there are two focal points in being, that of creator and creation; both essentially one. These two focal points are perpetually involved in a downward and upward movement of attraction. This is the force of love that is the cause of our existence; it is the secret of creation.

The condensed idea
Everything is finite, except God

12 Adam and Eve

The story of Adam's creation is announced as a turning point in the destiny of Earth itself. Adam and Eve are central to the story of human creation and human vocation. Adam is the first human being, the first prophet, the first being with knowledge. God makes Adam from clay, teaches him the names of everything, completes him by breathing life into him and calls him his *khalifa*, 'vicegerent on Earth' (Q2:30).

Adam is the first human being and is 'fashioned in the best of images' (Q40:64). God has spent time on the formation and image of man and God distinguishes man from other beings by breathing into him of his own spirit; thus, man comes into the fullness of his being only through that final breath. Exactly what is meant by *khalifa* in this context is open to interpretation in similar ways to the biblical *Imago Dei*, except that *khalifa* does imply some kind of successor or representative who will settle on Earth. Adam and the sons of Adam are being entrusted to look after the Earth.

DOUBTING ANGELS

Man has been created from a clot of blood, yet it is not man's biology that distinguishes him, but his intellectual and spiritual properties. Man has been predetermined to have knowledge, and it is this knowledge that designates him a place at the top of creation's hierarchy. Adam is, then, the first human being (*bashar*), but news of his creation is not met with eagerness by God's pre-existing creatures. When the angels question God as to why he is creating a being who will only cause bloodshed on Earth,

TIMELINE

6TH CENTURY BCE	1508–12
First draft of Pentateuch (Torah) emerges	Michelangelo paints Sistine Chapel with image depicting creation of Adam

God's reply is 'I know what you do not know.' Early commentaries on the Qur'an attributed this bloodshed by man, not as bloodshed to be caused by Adam himself, but by the descendants of Adam who, later on, will not follow God's law.

God's repsonse to the angels is to test them. He asks them to name what is around them, but they do not have this knowledge and realize the error of their question. Adam, however, does know the names of all things, because God has taught him already. It is this knowledge of all things animate and inanimate that distinguishes him from what has been created before him. Thus, the angels prostrate themselves in response to God's command and in recognition of Adam's superiority. The only angel that fails to do so is Iblis, a jinn or angel who is made of fire and considers himself superior to Adam. Iblis becomes the 'accursed satan' (see Chapter 18).

Iqbal and the fall

Some Muslim thinkers saw a positive ray in the first human act of disobedience. One of the few Muslim theologians of the modern period who has tried to reconcile a good God with the existence of moral and natural evil, was the Indian philosopher-poet Muhammad Iqbal.

Iqbal saw the creation of man as the creation of a being who, driven by desire and passion, would tear away all veils. For Iqbal, Adam's transgression was not a loss and 'not an act of moral depravity: it is man's transition from simple consciousness to the first flash of self-consciousness, a kind of waking from the dream of nature'. For Iqbal, good and evil fall within the same whole of creation because both are predicated on God's risk-taking, faith in humanity and human freedom to choose.

ADAM'S SLIP

The story in this passage tells us that Adam and his wife, who remains nameless in the Qur'an, are both commanded by God to live in paradise. But Adam, too, is tested. He is told to eat whatever he wishes, but to stay away from a certain tree, lest he transgress. There are varying opinions as to what kind of tree, but the Qur'an refers to it as a 'tree of eternity' (*shajarat al-khuld*; Q20:120). But Adam is tempted to eat from the tree through Iblis's

1667

Publication of Milton's *Paradise Lost*

1930

Muhammad Iqbal explores Qur'anic creation story

intervention, an action that is termed a *zalla* – a 'slip' – and both Adam and his partner are ejected from paradise. The Qur'anic story does not impute any blame on Eve for Adam's mistake.

In the story of Adams' creation, and his eating from the 'tree of knowledge', Adam's first act of disobedience is also his first act of human freedom. While Adam is forgiven by God, this story is an example of how, in practically every religion, culture and philosophical tradition, humans eventually become estranged or alienated from a god/gods or a bountiful nature. The Qur'anic story is about the fall of Iblis, who refused to bow before Adam, rather than the fall of man. Thus, the Qur'an distinguishes between humanity's loss of a certain state and human loss as our earthly existential paradigm. Man's first slip leads to his expulsion from paradise, but the Earth is also sacred territory, the cycle and rhythm of nature are also the signs of God and man's deliverance from loss to success lie in following divine guidance.

DEFINING 'SOUL'

The story of Adam and Eve is also the story of the first man and woman. Men and women are physically and emotionally connected to one another in all kinds of ways and language, sex and sexuality are essential to this connection. As the Qur'an says, 'O Mankind, keep your duty to your Lord who created you from a single soul and from it created its mate and spread from these many men and women' (Q4:1). The primal couple, Adam and Eve begin their lives in paradise amid the new physical creation, but their relational, spiritual and moral lives are fulfilled only on Earth.

In recent years some Muslim feminists have argued that the word 'soul', as in 'from a single soul', is conceptually neither male nor female (even though it is feminine, grammatically). There is no linguistic justification to attribute maleness to soul and, therefore, for assuming that this original soul is that of Adam. From this perspective, the word 'Adam' in the Qur'an functions generally as a collective noun referring to the human, rather than to a male human being.

Eve is a mystery

The Qur'an speaks of Adam and his wife in several verses. Eve or Hawwa, as she is known in Islam, is not mentioned in the Qur'an by name, nor is she seen as responsible for tempting Adam to eat from the tree. There is one *hadith* that mentions her name in relation to her creation from man's body. Adam called her Hawwa because she is created from a living thing (*hayy*). In the *Stories of the Prophets*, there is a beautiful story of the creation of Eve, whom God first calls his own 'handmaiden', but whom he gifts to Adam at Adam's request as long as Adam will take her in trust and thanks.

Thus, the argument is that the Qur'an uses other words such as *bashar* and *al-insan* to talk of human beings and the word Adam is used and retained more as a concept than an actual name of a particular human being. For some Sufis, including Ibn al-`Arabi, Eve is the hidden aspect of Adam through which he knows himself, where the feminine completes the masculine.

Adam's transgression is not a repeated theme in the Qur'an, nor is he set up as the origin of all subsequent human wrongdoing, because Adam is already forgiven for his slip. Adam and Eve must now experience distance from God, in order to understand what nearness was.

The condensed idea
Adam was the first prophet and the father of mankind

13 Jesus

Islam is the only religion outside Christianity in which Jesus is really present both in the Qur'an and in Islamic thought. But Jesus is not central to Islam's understanding of God in the same way that he is to Christianity. The Qur'anic story of Jesus is about Jesus the prophet, not Jesus as God's son, Jesus the saviour or Jesus the Messiah.

Islam makes reference to Christianity in various ways, but it lays emphasis on scripture and prophecy as defining modes of God's revelation. By contrast, scripture and prophecy play a secondary role in Christianity in the sense that, through Jesus Christ, God no longer offers us a prophetic message pointing to an eschatological reality, but rather offers himself – it is the Incarnation that is central to Christian theology. The Qur'an makes several references to Jesus, as if 'correcting' an audience, 'Christ Jesus, the son of Mary was no more than a messenger of Allah and his word, which he bestowed on Mary and a spirit proceeding from him. Say not three it will be better for you Allah is one God.' (Q4:171). These verses have usually been seen as doctrinal rejections of the Trinity and Jesus's divinity.

'SPIRIT OF GOD'
Jesus's divinity is central to any Christian Christology, in which his life, death and resurrection structure man's relationship with God. Islam does not have this Christology central to its doctrine of God, but it does have a Christology of sorts, because the Qur'an speaks of Jesus in multiple ways. In the Qur'an, there are more than 100 allusions to Christian doctrine, Christians

TIMELINE

3RD CENTURY CE	**4TH CENTURY CE**	**7TH–8TH CENTURY**
Doctrine of Trinity emerges	Arian controversy	Earliest responses by Christians to the rise of Islam

(*Nasara*) and Muslim attitudes towards them as communities of believers. Jesus or `Isa, as he is called in the Qur'an, is mentioned in 15 chapters of the work and in 93 verses, using the words 'sign' 'mercy' or 'example'. For Muslims, Jesus is a revered prophet in the whole historical chain of prophets. It is Jesus, not Muhammad, who will be the returning messenger of end times. He is born of Mary whom the Qur'an describes as chaste and pure, with Islam affirming Mary's immaculate conception and the virginal birth. In the Qur'an, Jesus is also described as prophet, word and messenger of God. Even though there is no one particular Jesus narrative that brings together the Christic, miraculous and prophetic nature of Jesus under his most dramatic epithet, 'spirit of God' (*Ruh-Allah*); this epithet nevertheless defines Jesus as one chosen by God in both Islamic and Christian belief.

INDEED, THE FREE SPIRITS OF ISLAMIC MYSTICISM FOUND IN THE MAN JESUS, NOT ONLY THE EXAMPLE OF PIETY, LOVE AND ASCETICISM, WHICH THEY SOUGHT TO EMULATE, BUT ALSO THE CHRIST WHO EXEMPLIFIES FULFILLED HUMANITY, A HUMANITY ILLUMINED BY GOD.

Mahmoud Ayoub, 'Towards an Islamic Christology'

CHRIST'S CRUCIFIXION

If Christianity begins with the death and resurrection of Jesus, the Qur'an seemingly denies his death:

[The Jews] saying: 'We killed Christ Jesus the son of Mary, the messenger of God.' And they did not kill him, and they did not crucify him, but it was made to appear so to them [shubbiha lahum]. And those who have differed about it are in doubt about it: they do not have knowledge about it, but only the following of supposition. They did not kill him for certain. (Q4:157)

This is the only verse in the Qur'an that mentions the crucifixion of Jesus. Some Muslims, including Muhammad Abduh and Rashid Rida, rejected the view that Jesus was taken up from this world without dying. They maintained that Jesus did die on the cross, but that his soul was taken up to heaven. The issue is that, even if Muslims came to believe

9TH CENTURY	**16TH CENTURY**	**19TH/20TH CENTURIES**
Intense discussions between Christians and Muslims on the nature of Jesus	Martin Luther's defence of Christianity against the Turks	Christian missionaries travel to Muslim lands

Jesus and Sufism

While the Incarnation and divinity of Jesus continued to be a contested topic between Sunni orthodox Muslims and Christians, not all Muslims saw the Trinity as a doctrine that divided God's unity. In the world of poetry and Sufi spirituality; it is important to note that Jesus was given a particularly important place. The great Andalusian mystic, poet and philosopher Ibn al-`Arabi (1165-1240) and other Persian Sufi poets saw the Trinity and the Incarnation as symbolic ways of speaking about the Absolute. For Ibn al-`Arabi, number did not beget multiplicity in the Divine substance. He wrote in his famous poem, '*Tarjuman al-Ashwaq*' ('The Translator of Desires'): 'My beloved is three although he is One, Even as the three persons are made one Person in essence'.

that Jesus did die on the cross before he was raised, in the Qur'anic frame of references, this death has no atoning significance and would not be seen as the decisive event in the redemptive plan for humankind.

That Jesus has a non-salvific role, yet is particularly revered as a prophet with the epithet 'spirit of God', means that Jesus can be viewed as both a bridge and a gulf between Christianity and Islam.

DIVIRGENT SCHOOLS OF THOUGHT

For centuries apologetics, or polemics, have shaped the discourse between Muslims and Christians. In simple terms, Muhammad, his prophecy and the Qur'anic verses on Jesus and Mary and the Gospels have been regarded as either a heresy or a challenge to Christianity. From the Muslim perspective, Jesus is the seal of the Israelite prophets but Muhammad is the seal of all prophets. Jesus remains a precursor to Muhammad, even though it is Jesus who will return to Earth in his second coming. Christianity was true in its primordial message of God's absolute oneness and transcendence – Christians had distorted this truth by straying completely and ascribing a divine nature to a human prophet. From the Islamic perspective, the crucifixion and Trinity are not seen through the prism of either kenotic or relational love, but largely as errors in Christian understanding of a distorted gospel and a deified Christ.

However, Muslim reflections on the life and ministry of Jesus are not monolithic and, outside the doctrinal differences and polemical debates, Jesus has been understood in a variety of ways within the various Islamic intellectual and literary disciplines. Mystical poetry such as that of the 13th-century Turkish Persian mystic and poet/theologian, Jalal al-Din Rumi, gives different images for Jesus and Christianity. Considering Jesus to be less a saviour and Son of God and more a Muslim prophet, Rumi sees him as the smiling prophet and much more than a miracle worker.

As a prophet, Jesus represents the 'perfection of humanity', a concept in which the attributes of God are manifest. In his *Mathnawi*, Rumi saw that logic and intellect were limited in their ability to inspire humanity to any great endeavour. It was the prophets and seers – people of no formal knowledge – who captured the hearts of those they met and Jesus was among these people:

> The myriad of Pharaoh's lances were shattered by Moses with a single staff. Myriads were the therapeutic arts of Galen; before Jesus and his life-giving breath they were a laughing stock. Myriads were the books of pre-Islamic poems; at the word of an illiterate prophet they were put to shame.

Jesus's suffering

The impact of the cross is not simply that of a visual image; it represents a truth that is both terrible and hopeful – death and triumph. The various meanings of the cross still point to the one truth that the passion and death of Christ remain at the centre of the Christian faith. The cross is the very focus of its sacramental anamnesis in "the bread and wine" of the Eucharist. Nothing in Islam compares to this. If anything, many Muslim thinkers saw the suffering on the cross as the ultimate flaw in Christian belief, namely, that the religion focused too much on human suffering and brokenness and less on a human spirit that feels drawn towards God rather than requiring reconciliation with God.

The condensed idea
Islamic Christology begins with Jesus as the 'spirit of God'

14 Abraham

Abraham is a central figure in Judaism, Christianity and Islam and is known as the father of the Semites. Mentioned 69 times in the Qur'an he is second only to Moses in this respect. Abraham is also unique in being given the honorific title, the 'close friend' (*khalil*) of God (Q4:125).

Abraham is depicted in the Qur'an as a prophet who, from a very early age, had problems trying to understand God and trying to discover God. He was restless and knew, perhaps, the pagan environment in which he lived did not have the answers. Ultimately, Abraham knew that God was not in the stars or the wind, neither was he the Sun or the Moon or any of the forces he could see. God was in something else.

ABRAHAM'S MONOTHEISM

This aspect of Abraham's belief is captured in the concept of *hanif*. The Qur'an presents Abraham as a *hanif* – that is, the bearer of a primordial and pristine monotheism. Islamic thought holds that this primal Abrahamic belief, called the *hanifiyya*, gradually became corrupted and fragmented in later years by Abraham's progeny. Abraham therefore functions as a spiritual precursor to Islam, with Muhammad's revelation seen as God's means of restoring this original monotheism.

Abraham is also seen as the genealogical father of the Arabs, who trace their lineage from Abraham's son, Ishmael. Muslim tradition narrates how

TIMELINE

14000 BCE	4400 BCE
Origins of monotheism	Age of Abraham

this belief in Abraham's lineage that was prevalent throughout pre-Islamic Arabia, and scholars note this perhaps lends an extra polemical tone to the Qur'an's presentation of Abraham as a standard-bearer of upright monotheism.

ABRAHAM IN MUSLIM HISTORY

Abraham is a central figure in Muslim sacred history. According to tradition, by the command of God, Abraham left his concubine Hagar and son Ishmael in Arabia with bare provisions. In search of water, Hagar ran seven times between the two hills of Safa and Marwah but could not find any water. With Hagar in despair, the angel Jibril (Gabriel) hit the ground with his wing, from which a water fountain sprang forth. Muslims travel between these two hills during the *hajj* and *umrah* pilgrimage rites (see Chapter 25), as a commemoration of God's reward for Hagar's patience.

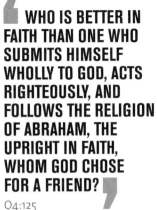

WHO IS BETTER IN FAITH THAN ONE WHO SUBMITS HIMSELF WHOLLY TO GOD, ACTS RIGHTEOUSLY, AND FOLLOWS THE RELIGION OF ABRAHAM, THE UPRIGHT IN FAITH, WHOM GOD CHOSE FOR A FRIEND?

Q4:125

In one of the most important features of Muslim history, the tradition credits Abraham with rebuilding the Kaaba after it was damaged during the great flood of Noah. Muslims believe Abraham constructed the Kaaba in its present shape, and that the Black Stone, located in the far corner of the Kaaba, is the sole remaining feature from the time of Abraham.

ABRAHAM'S STORY

The story of Abraham is found across many Qur'anic verses. The most dominant theme in the narrative is that of Abraham's battles against the idolatry of his father and the wider community. Abraham famously smashes idols, an event that is recorded in two places in the Qur'an (Q21:52–5; Q37:90–4). God then miraculously saves him from the punishment of a burning fire, one of several miracles with which Abraham is associated. Perhaps the most famous Qur'anic story is that of Abraham's willing

800–300 BCE

Axial Age

570 CE

Birth of Muhammad

sacrifice of his son, who is unnamed in the Qur'an, but identified as Ishmael in later Muslim tradition. As in the biblical tale, God intervenes through the angel Jibril, to inform Abraham that his sacrifice has already been accepted. There is an important difference, however, in that Abraham's son is not deceived about the act and willingly submits himself:

Abraham and the idols

Abraham's submission to God is a significant feature of his life, and yet he is also of great interest as a figure, because he is depicted in the Qur'an as somebody who, from a very early age, was searching for God. He expressed a daily restlessness and a resistance to the idea that God might lie in powerful forces like the stars or the Sun or the wind or the Moon. For him, God must lie in something else.

Abraham always asked his father who made the wooden idols he sold in his shop. He asked him why he worshipped such statues. Abraham insisted that the only true God was the one who made the heavens and the Earth. On one occasion he smashed all the idols except for one large one. When his family returned and were angry to see their gods all broken, they asked him who had done this. Abraham replied, 'It is that big one who did it. Go ask them, if they can speak.' His father and everyone else knew that the idol could not speak but they were still angry at his impudence. They did not listen to him when he pleaded with them to stop worshipping false gods, who had no power, and to turn to the one true God.

The polytheists begin to shout that Abraham should be burnt but he was saved by God. And so it is Abraham's instinctive faith and belief that God resides in the unseen and shows mercy to all who turn to him that becomes the guiding force in his life.

And when he reached with him [the age of] exertion, he said, 'O my son, indeed I have seen in a dream that I [must] sacrifice you, so see what you think.' He said, 'O my father, do as you are commanded. You will find me, if Allah wills, of the steadfast.' And when they had both submitted and he put him down upon his forehead, We called to him, 'O Abraham, You have fulfilled the vision.' Indeed, We thus reward the doers of good; indeed, this was the clear trial. (Q37:102–106)

This story provides the scriptural basis behind the Muslim *Eid al-Adha* festival. Muslim families gather to sacrifice a sheep or goat and perform prayers and almsgiving, as a way of commemorating Abraham's willingness to submit to God.

THE IDEA OF AN ABRAHAMIC RELIGION

Today, the figure of Abraham has assumed a renewed relevance owing to his status as the father of Judaism, Christianity and Islam. He is regarded as the unifying figure, the father of the Semites and a figure of hospitality in interreligious encounters. Revered as the patriarch of the monotheistic religions, the biblical and Qur'anic stories of Abraham's welcoming of strangers and guests (Genesis 18:1–10 and Q51:24–30) are understood by many as an example of his selflessness and openness.

In an age of religious diversity and with increased focus on the importance of interreligious dialogue, much has been made of the shared Abrahamic roots of Judaism, Christianity and Islam. The notion of Abrahamic religions is often presented as a means of building mutual understanding and emphasizing a common religious heritage.

Yet the term 'Abrahamic' is itself contested. Voices within each tradition object to the term on the grounds that it threatens to blur the essential doctrinal differences between each tradition. Several American evangelical figures publicly denounce the term as emblematic of the threat of an increasingly visible, assertive and politicized form of Islam in the public sphere.

Moreover, the popular use of the Abrahamic label disguises how the descriptions of Abraham as a *hanif* in the Qur'an are often used in direct contradistinction to Jewish and Christian ancestral claims. The Qur'an states, 'Abraham was neither a Jew nor a Christian, but he was one inclining towards truth, a Muslim (Q3:67). The Islamic view of prophecy sees Abraham, like all prophets, as a 'muslim' prophet before revelation finds its final expression in the Qur'an and prophecy of Muhammad. In fact, the Qur'an also calls Islam 'the religion (*milla*) of your father Abraham (Q22:78). While Abraham is symbolic of the common ancestry of monotheism, he remains a powerful and contested prophet.

The condensed idea
Abraham always knew that there is only one God

15 Angels

Belief in angels is a tenet of the Islamic faith. The Arabic word *malak* (*mala'ik*) means 'messenger' and the Qur'an uses the term, and variants of it, 99 times. The most prominent angel in Islam is Jibril (Gabriel) even though he is never given the appellation of 'angel' in the Qur'an. Angels are made of light and, unlike human beings, do not have free will. But they are essential to the Qur'anic themes of creation, revelation, prophecy and eschatology.

Belief in angels is a necessary aspect of faith (*iman*) in Islam. The Qur'an says, 'Whoever is an enemy to God and his angels and His messengers and Jibril and Mikail (Michael), then indeed God is an enemy to the disbelievers' (Q2:97). There is also a famous *hadith* in which Jibril asks the Prophet about the different stages of belief. The first stage is Islam, which is to testify that there is no deity worthy of worship except God and that Muhammad is his messenger. This stage also requires observance of the five pillars of Islam (see page 88). The second stage is *iman*, which is to 'believe in God and his angels and his books and his messengers and in the Last Day, and in fate (*qadar*), both in its good and in its evil aspects'.

APPEARING AS HUMANS

Angels are described as 'messengers with wings' but they cannot be seen because they are heavenly beings. They can, however, take on different forms, including the human. An example of this occurs during the

TIMELINE

4TH CENTURY CE	610 CE
Church Fathers agree on different forms of angels	Jibril brings first revelation to Muhammad

annunciation of Mary when Jibril is sent to Mary in the form of a man: 'And she took, in seclusion from them, a screen. Then we sent to her our angel, and he represented himself to her as a perfect man'(Q19:17). While the word *ruh* means spirit, it is often translated as angel in this context, thus engendering a close relationship between spirt, angel and Jibril.

In another passage, it is angels who deliver the news of Jesus to Mary: 'And when the angels said, "Mary, God has chosen you, and purified you; he has chosen you above all the women of the world" (Q3:42). The connection between spirit, soul, angels and divine command also appear in several Qur'anic passages. such as 'They will question you concerning the spirit. Say: "The spirit comes from the command of my Lord". You have been given very little knowledge' (Q17:85). This command is associated with the 'Preserved Tablet' the source of all books, from which the spirit is brought by the angels to the heart of the Prophet.

> **❝ THEN THE MAN READ AND WHEN HE DID, THE ANGEL BOWED. IT WAS AS IF HE HAD ALWAYS BEEN READING AND NOW WAS ABLE TO OBEY AND BRING TO PASS. ❞**
> Rainer Maria Rilke (1875–1926)

AIDING MUHAMMAD

There are various stories in the Qur'an in which angels feature as agents either preparing or helping the Prophet in his mission. This includes traditions surrounding the Prophet's night journey from Mecca to Jerusalem and then his ascent into the heavens. Another famous incident is related about the Prophet in which, while he was tending sheep, two men dressed in white came upon him with a golden basin of snow. They opened his breast, took his heart and stirred their hands inside. Muhammad explained that these men were angels who had extracted a black speck from his heart and then washed his heart with the snow to cleanse it thoroughly. In other words, Muhammad had been chosen and prepared to receive revelation from an early age.

621 CE	**8TH CENTURY CE**
Jibril brings Buraq to Muhammad, and the story of the ascension	Belief in angels stated; Abu Hanifa's creed

ANGELS AND THE CREATION

Other than the prominent role of Jibril, perhaps the most famous story relating to angels is in the story of human creation. The Qur'an says:

> 'Behold', the Lord said to the angels, 'I will create a vicegerent on Earth.' They said, 'Will you place therein one who will make mischief therein and shed blood? Whilst we do celebrate your praises and glorify your holy name?' He said, 'I know what you know not'. And he taught Adam the names of all things; then he placed them before the angels and said, 'tell me the names of these things if you are right'. They said, 'Glory to you of knowledge, we have none save what you have taught us; in truth it is you who are perfect in knowledge and wisdom'. He said, 'Oh Adam, tell them their names'. When he had told them their names, God said, 'Did I not tell you that I know the secrets of heaven and Earth, and I know what you reveal and what you conceal?' And behold, we said to the angels: 'Bow down to Adam and they bowed down: not so Iblis; he refused and was haughty: he was of those who reject faith'. (Q2: 30–34)

It is this story that seals humankind at the top of creation's hierarchy and reveals the moment at which the angels understand their nature, purpose and limitations. They know their singular purpose is to glorify God, but that Adam's knowledge means that Adam has been created for a different purpose in life, which only God knows.

ANGELS IN ISLAM

When looking to see how angels and their responsibilities are described, there are resonances with the Judeo-Christian tradition. Nevertheless, a fairly distinct angelology appears in the way the Qur'an and the *hadith* literature mention specific angels by name.

Angels feature quite largely in Islamic eschatology, the cataclysmic end of the created order. Amongst the most notable are Israfil, the angel who will blow the trumpet and signal the coming of the Day of Judgement. Mikhail is the angel who provides nourishment as well as being responsible for bringing rain and thunder to Earth. Finally, Izra'il is the angel of death and it is said that Izra'il acts only as God's instrument and does not know who will die until the tree beneath God's throne drops a leaf with the person's name on it.

Angels and Sufis

In hagiographical literature, we find that angels often serve as instruments of God's care and protection for the young Sufi destined very early on in his life to follow a particular mystical path (see Chapter 41). The mystic may be frightened in his ignorance but is always learning the truth from this powerful presence. One of the most powerful saints and scholars Abdul Qadir al-Jilani wrote:

When I was a small child, every day I was visited by an angel in the shape of a beautiful young man. He would walk with me from our house to school and make the children in the class give me a place in the front row. He would stay with me the whole day and then bring me back home. I would learn in a single day more than the other students learned in a week. I did not know who he was. One day I asked him and he said, 'I am one of Allah's angels. He sent me to you and asked me to be with you as long as you study'.

Every time I felt a desire to go and play with other children I would hear a voice saying, 'Come to Me instead, O blessed one, come to Me'. In terror I would go and seek the comfort of my mother's arms. Now even in my most intense devotions and long seclusions, I cannot hear that voice clearly.
Abdul Qadir al-Jilani, *The Secret of Secrets*, xiv

The condensed idea
Angels gather in places where God is remembered

16 Heaven

God is described as the 'Lord of the Heavens and Earth' in the Qur'an, and his creation of the visible and the hidden world are proofs of his majesty. The promise of heaven is central for all Muslims and, for many, it is the hope of this physical abode that drives daily prayers, almsgiving, fasting and the other rituals and regulations that are central to religious life.

The delights and rewards of heaven are described in very physical terms and Islamic texts refer to several layers of heaven for those whom God rewards. Within these heavens is the abode of paradise, variously referred to as 'the garden' (*janna*), 'gardens' (*jannat*), and by its title, *Firdaus*.

THE SPIRITUAL AND THE SENSUAL

The Qur'an makes frequent reference to the pleasures of paradise as a tool to encourage belief and good conduct in mankind. The Islamic paradise is a place of both spiritual and sensual reward. Spiritually, paradise is described as a place of God's pleasure, forgiveness and protection. It is here that God thanks believers for what they patiently endured in their worldly life (Q76:12). Sensual descriptions of heaven depict paradise as a place of flowing rivers of milk and honey, non-intoxicating wine, the shade of trees, young boy servants, garments of silk, and luscious fruits and foods. (Q76:12–22)

While most see these as clear incitements to lead a disciplined religious life, the female Sufi mystic Rabi'a of Basra (d. 801) famously saw these as obstacles to the true worship of God:

TIMELINE

2400 BCE	610–32 CE
Book of the Dead, funerary manuscripts dating back to the Egyptian Old Kingdom	Qur'an contains numerous references to heaven as a place in an afterlife

O God! If I worship you for fear of hell,
burn me in hell
and if I worship you in hope of paradise,
exclude me from paradise.
But if I worship you for your own sake,
grudge me not your everlasting beauty

On the basis of these sensory descriptions of paradise found in the Qur'an and expounded in traditional writings, it is often said that Islam conceives of an *afterworld*, as opposed to the *afterlife* of Christianity. This has been a source of controversy. For some, the Islamic heaven was simply too sensual to be a spiritual reward. Several Christian thinkers contrasted the high spirituality of the Christian message with what was considered an appeal to lower, baser instincts in the Islamic message. See the words of the ninth-century Arab Christian al-Kindy:

Heaven's existence

The Arabic *al-sam'* denotes sky or roof and in the feminine form, sky or heaven. The Qur'an mentions the plural, *samawat*, 190 times. According to the Qur'an, God first created all that belongs to Earth and then created the seven heavens. Heaven was originally smoke, but God created seven heavens in two days. At the beginning, God's throne was on the waters; then God elevated his throne to the seventh heaven (Q23:86). However, in another verse, God's chair contains the heavens and the Earth (Q2:225). What we know in terms of planets and constellations of stars belong to the lower heavens.

All these [descriptions of paradise in the Qur'an] suit only stupid, ignorant and simple-minded people, who are inexperienced and unfamiliar with reading texts and understanding old traditions, and who are just a rabble of rough Bedouins accustomed to eating desert lizards and chameleons.

The language of wine, drinking and intoxication are present throughout the narratives of heaven. Islamic thought is not apologetic about the heavenly fulfilment of human physical desires. Creation is to be enjoyed through the senses because sensual pleasures, far from being associated with primeval

725 CE

Heofon in *Beowulf* translates as 'sky'

1000

Heofon used in Christian sense to mean a place where God dwells

Heaven's promise

We must experience being earthly before we can assume the heavenly. The heavenly is the fulfilment of all the desires that remain in us, but most significantly the vision of God. Themes and images of heaven are repeated in various ways, but the descriptions always convey indulgence without sin. These depictions of heavenly bliss are not activities of entertainment or hedonism, but are instead about reward, for there is no escaping the Qur'anic exhortation that life after death makes distinctions between good and bad. God may forgive everyone everything, but heaven and hell provide difficult, yet seductive, ways of thinking about right and wrong in this life. This immortal life, evoked in both sensual and spiritual terms, is based on God's promises, but it is the promise of God himself that is the ultimate heavenly reward: 'On that day, some faces will be radiant, gazing upon their Lord' (Q75:22–23).

sin or redemption, are part of God's creation and, therefore, divine blessings. The spiritual and the carnal coexist. Yet, all these pleasures pale into insignificance when compared to the possible vision of God. This is the real reward, where expectation will rise to ecstasy.

The Qu'ran mentions seven layers of heaven (Q41:12, 65:12, 67:3–4) and the most famous and vivid descriptions of these are to be found in the famous ascension (*mi`raj*) story. It is said that, early into his prophethood, Muhammad travelled from Mecca to Jerusalem on the back of a winged horse, named *Buraq*. From Jerusalem, Muhammad ascended and travelled through the seven layers of heaven, meeting previous prophets, including Joseph, Abraham, Jesus and Moses. This culminated in meeting God on reaching the highest (seventh) layer of heaven. Muslims have read this story differently, both as a literal, physical experience and as an esoteric, spiritual experience of Muhammad's. This heavenly journey is seen as confirming Muhammad's prophecy, and also the significance of Jerusalem in Islamic thought as the gateway to heaven. To this day, the night of the ascension (*lailat al-mi`raj*) is one of the most important fixtures in the Muslim calendar.

Islamic thought holds that entry into heaven is conditional upon the believer possessing a clean, pure heart, free of sins, at the point of death. This lends great weight to the concept of repentance (*tawbah*) for worldly sins. The famous medieval scholar al-Ghazali (d. 1111) likens the human heart to a shiny, glass surface. Sins are like a stain upon glass; a stain that can only be rubbed off by sincere repentance to the all-merciful and forgiving God. Heaven is therefore understood as the reward for a life of repentance, rather than moral perfection, which is beyond our human capacity.

> ON EARTH THERE IS NO HEAVEN BUT THERE ARE PIECES OF IT.
>
> Jules Renard (1864–1910)

HEAVENLY REWARDS

The list of specifically meritorious acts that are rewarded with heaven is quite long in the scriptural sources, and includes prayer, almsgiving and respect for parents, among others. In the Islamic tradition, heaven became especially infused with the idea of martyrdom in defense of the faith. A famous Qur'anic verse says 'Do not think those who are killed in the way of God are dead. Rather, they are alive, with their Lord, and they have provision' (Q3:186). Classical thinkers wrote that martyrs could immediately enter heaven after death, and thus be spared the intervening period of 'punishment in the grave'. Some claim that, according to Muslim tradition, those killed on the battlefield defending Islam would be buried immediately on the spot, waiving the usual death and funeral rites, as their place in heaven was considered already guaranteed. The glorification of the martyr reaches its apogee in the *hadith* collections, and at times this is described in explicitly sexual terms, most famously in the traditions that speak of 72 wives, or virgins, awaiting the martyr.

Despite such explicitly sensual terms that appeal solely to male sensibilities, Muslim feminist writers argue that the apparent Qur'anic silence on the sensual rewards awaiting female believers in no way constitutes a denial for the female believers. They argue that the Qur'an is spiritually egalitarian and that traditional texts simply describe heaven, literally or metaphorically, in terms that would capture its inevitably male audience.

The condensed idea
Death is the continuation of our journey to God

17 Hell

The whole of human history is a movement from creation to the eschaton, or the afterlife. Death, the grave, resurrection, the Day of Judgement and the afterlife are Qur'anic themes reminding us not only of earthly transience, but of a final destiny with God. All Muslims hope to spend their eternal lives in heaven/paradise (*jannat*) as opposed to hell or more accurately hellfire (*jahannam*).

Heaven and hell are prominent themes, depicted in graphic visual imagery in the Qur'an, which states repeatedly that on the Day of Judgement, everyone will know their fate. The relationship between this life and the afterworld lies in accepting that there is a place in time that has yet to occur; it is often depicted in terms of paradise or hell, or garden and fire, but it is all-pervasive; this other world can be imagined but it is not imaginary.

A WORLD OF SUFFERING

Hell destines one to both physical and spiritual suffering, and the language of blazing fires, scalding water and iron maces creates a terrifying image. The inhabitants of hell will curse and blame each other and will find no one to defend or intercede on their behalf. The most common term, occurring 125 times in the Qur'an, is 'the fire' (*al-Nar*); the next is the title *jahannam*, found in 77 verses. The different names led Muslim thinkers to develop a distinct topography of hell, with each name referring to one of seven layers of hell, or to each of its seven gates (Q15:43–44). The descriptions of hell found in later Muslim thought and

TIMELINE

2100 BCE	400 BCE	610–32 CE
Epic of Gilgamesh contains references to a netherworld	Plato's Gorgias refers to Tartarus as a place for punishment after death	Qur'an contains several references to the fire/hell

the *hadith* collections further develop the Qur'anic images. Various heinous forms of punishment that are not mentioned in the Qur'an include being trampled on by angels.

SUFFERING ETERNALLY

Not all Muslims and scholars agree as to the exact nature of hell. Is it an eternal destination or are some, even all, of the condemned eventually forgiven and allowed to enter paradise? One highly debated issue in classical Islam concerned the eternality of hell. The mainstream position was that hell, like heaven, was eternal. This was based of Qur'anic verses that clearly refer to those 'abiding eternally therein' (Q3:88). The idea was contested, however.

Muslim scholars of the rationalist school, known as the Mu`tazila, struggled with the idea of another eternal essence operating alongside God, and had their own arsenal of Qur'anic verses to support their position, such as 'everything shall perish except his face' (Q28:88).

Even from within the mainstream Sunni tradition, famous thinkers such as Ibn Taymiyyah (d. 1328) held the view that hell itself will be extinguished at the end of time, at which point all souls will be reunited with God. This owed much to the ethical problem of an infinite punishment for finite sins, especially in lieu of the famous *hadith* in which God declares, 'Indeed, my mercy exceeds my wrath'. Among the ways in which mainstream Islamic thought resolved this issue, was to distinguish between the eternality of

Repentance and hell

Despite the call to worship and human accountability for its own actions in the Qur'an, there is a recognition that humankind is created both weak and strong, both discerning and ignorant. Human beings are always open to temptation – the cycle of wrongdoing followed by repentance is present in the concept of *tawba* or 'returning' to God. God, for his part acting in accordance with his merciful nature, will always forgive. This does not mean that God is not also a God of judgement or the avenger of evils committed. But if God has any weakness, then that weakness must be human repentance.

725 CE

The words *hel* and *helle* exist, referring to a lower world

14TH CENTURY

Dante's *Divine Comedy* describes a journey through hell

hell itself and man's time spent there – allowing for the soul's eventual entry into heaven after an appropriate time of expiation in hell.

HELL'S PUNISHMENTS

Another key problem relating to hell is how to interpret these vivid descriptions of the punishments in the hereafter. Are these to be taken literally, denoting physical punishment in a geographical, spatial abode? Or are they symbolic, implying a spiritual sense of punishment? Perhaps the most common view is that of man's bodily resurrection at the end of time and, with it, the physical reward or punishment as described in the Qur'an (while maintaining that events of the hereafter belong to the realm of the unseen [ghayb] and thus cannot be compared exactly to our present, sensory experiences). The famous Indian Muslim philosopher Muhammad Iqbal denied the literal understanding of hell and its punishments saying that heaven and hell are human states, not localities; heaven and hell are about our triumph or failure.

> **THE PROPHET SAID 'WHOEVER SAYS, "NO ONE HAS THE RIGHT TO BE WORSHIPPED BUT ALLAH" AND HAS IN HIS HEART GOOD (FAITH) EQUAL TO THE WEIGHT OF AN ATOM WILL BE TAKEN OUT OF HELL.'**
>
> *Hadith*

HELL'S INHABITANTS

The Qur'an provides extensive lists of those who are destined to hell and the nature of their crimes. Some of these relate to one's religious orientation, and so hell is commonly described as the place for 'unbelievers', 'hypocrites' and 'polytheists'. In other verses, hell is for those with specific character traits, such as the arrogant (Q7:36), backbiters and gossipers (Q104:1) and those who fail to feed the poor and needy (Q90:14–15). Very few individuals are specifically condemned to hell in the Qur'an, the notable exceptions being the Prophet's unbelieving uncle, Abu Lahab and his wife, the wives of Noah and Lot and Cain.

Classical Islamic thinkers predominantly understood adherence to Islam as an essential criterion for salvation. Yet, there are a number of famous thinkers, including al-Ghazali (d. 1111), who argued that certain Jews, Christians and others will be spared hellfire on account of their 'living far away from the lands of Islam', and thus being ignorant of the prophetic proofs of Muhammad.

MODERN INTERPRETATIONS OF HELL

Today, in light of the new realities of social and religious pluralism and globalization, some modern Muslim thinkers have rejected classical understandings of hell and have reinterpreted the relevant Qur'anic verses, stressing that pluralism is part of God's will, and that only God can judge the eventual fate of the Muslim or the non-Muslim, no matter how evil or righteous they seem.

By far the dominant Qur'anic theme regarding human destiny is that God's mercy or wrath awaits us all. A God in waiting is a constant theme in the Qur'an. God's compassion may mean forgiveness for every person in the end – in response to an 'atom's weight of good' – but we must base our lives on the constant endeavour to be morally aware, to do right and to do good deeds. We are responsible for our own deeds and when death comes, we are alone in death, carrying into the grave and into the next life only ourselves and our actions.

Saved and damned

Muslim scholars differed as to whether the torments of hell were eternal. There were other questions, such as whether heaven and hell actually exist now and, if so, where are they located? Some commentators described how hell is reached. Heaven is elevated whereas hell is a pit. The Qur'an says that 'the sinners will see the fire and recognize that they are to fall into it and they will find no outlet' (Q18:53). Others discussed that even though there is a veil between heaven and hell, the inhabitants of each abode can call to each other. They compare their experiences, now realizing that God's promises were true. There are vivid images of those in hell begging those in heaven for water to drink, but they are refused. This adds to the potent physical images of the inhabitants of hell already burning, yet only able to drink boiling water (Q6:70).

The condensed idea
God's mercy is limitless in the face of human repentance

18 Satan

There are many figures that represent wrongdoing or evil in the Islamic tradition, and Satan is one of them. Prior to becoming Satan, he is known as Iblis, a jinn made of fire who worshipped God faithfully for thousands of years and rose to the rank of angel, but then declined to prostrate himself in front of Adam. For this act of disobedience, he was rejected by God, the very being he had worshipped. It was then that Iblis became the 'accursed Satan', a personification of temptation and evil.

In the Qur'anic story of Adam's creation (see Chapter 12) and his eating from the 'tree of eternity and possession' (Q20:120), Iblis plays a brief but significant role in his new guise as Satan. He succeeds in tempting Adam in paradise, and thus fulfilling the pact he has made with God, to lead humankind astray. It is Satan's agreement with God that he be allowed to 'whisper' constantly, to have the freedom to tempt humankind, as long as he is able – not as a challenge to God, but as a challenge to human goodness and to the goodness of God's creation. Several verses in the Qur'an reveal Satan's intentions:

> Then Satan whispered to them, 'Oh Adam, shall I lead you to the tree of eternity and a kingdom that does not waste away?' (Q20:120)

TIMELINE

4TH CENTURY CE	10TH CENTURY
Lucifer frequently used in Christian theology to refer to Satan	Al-Hallaj sees Satan as a true monotheist

Satan's own pledge:

> 'I will lead them astray and I will arouse in them desires and I will command them so that they slit the ears of cattle and I will command them so that they change God's creation.' So whoever takes Satan as a guide instead of God, he has certainly incurred a clear loss. (Q4:119)

The concept of 'whispering' evokes an image of Satan working through subtle deceit, playing on the vulnerability of human desires. Human freedom means Satan now has a potential audience. He himself cannot change God's creation on his own; he needs the weakness, vulnerability and the moral consciousness of humankind for creation to change. Iblis-turned-Satan showed Adam and his descendants the consequences of disobeying God so that they now know their real struggle is with God as much as it is with Satan. Neither Satan nor Adam can return to Edenic innocence. Adam begs God to show him how to avoid Satan's snares, to which God's response is 'Stretch forth your hands and call upon me, for I am near and responsive'.

Evil is banal

In 1951, Hannah Arendt wrote *The Origins of Totalitarianism*, in which her assessment of the regimes of Hitler and Stalin had led her to conclude that the evil of these regimes was a particularly 20th-century phenomenon, a 'radical evil that was beyond the pale of human sinfulness'. However, in 1961, when Arendt attended the trial of Nazi war criminal Adolf Eichmann, in Jerusalem, her perspective on evil changed. Arendt saw that evil deeds – even committed on a gigantic scale – could not necessarily be traced to a demonic person or ideology, that there was an ordinariness in people like Eichmann who had committed huge atrocities. From this she concluded in a work entitled, *Eichmann in Jerusalem: A Report on the Banality of Evil*, that there was indeed a banality of evil. Doing terrible things became normalized and systemized into everyday life.

THE HUMAN CAPACITY TO SIN

The problem as to whether God acted arbitrarily and why he allows Satan this freedom to act in the world, remains unresolved, yet it lies at the heart

13TH CENTURY

Rumi's *Mathnawi* portrays Satan as a true lover of God

1795

William Blake's painting, 'Satan Exulting over Eve'.

> **WITHOUT THE POWERS THAT IBLIS REPRESENTS, THERE COULD BE NO MORAL UNIVERSE. WE COULD NOT CHOOSE THE RIGHT, BECAUSE THERE COULD BE NO WRONG, WHEREBY THE RIGHT COULD BE DISTINGUISHED.**
> S. Murata and W. Chittick,
> *The Vision of Islam*

of the human condition. In the Qur'an Adam is forgiven by God, but in his one act of disobedience, humankind becomes destined to a life of moral choices. Evil becomes equivalent to the things we do to ourselves and to one another that go against the wishes of a good God. Whether it is called sin or wrongdoing, the existential paradigm in Islam is not that of a tragic fall or primordial sin, but the human capacity to commit all manner of sins. Sin is an act, not a state of being: it is the things we do.

GOOD VERSUS EVIL

The themes and discussions around the existence of evil in Islam are largely familiar problems for those who hold onto a conception of a good and omnipotent God. Followers of monotheistic religions struggle with the concept of the dualism of good and evil. They try to illustrate how evil functions in a monotheistic framework without impinging on God's omnipotence and without granting Satan an independent existence at the same time.

Muslim thinkers who did consider human wrongdoing, did not look at evil as the ultimate tragedy of creation or human suffering as an abstract entity in the world; they did not speak of evil in some pure state, because it is extremely difficult to define pure evil. Indeed, in his work, *The Reconstruction of Religious Thought in Islam*, the Indian poet and philosopher Muhammad Iqbal sees the consequence of Adam's transgression as a key step in human development:

> The fall does not mean any moral depravity; it is man's transition from simple consciousness to the first flash of self-consciousness, a kind of waking from the dream of nature.

Philosophers and theologians have tried to reconcile the inevitability of human wrongdoing and the necessity of divine forgiveness in the face of a merciful and benign Creator.

SATAN, THE VICTIM

The Satan motif is a complex and comprehensive literary figure across religious traditions. The question as to what caused Iblis – who had worshipped God for thousands of years – suddenly to transform into Satan, the accursed, has no definitive answer in religious traditions. It is a problem of both pride and disobedience. Satan represents the destructive power of evil and destroys himself and others through his commitment to evil. Yet he is also a rebel figure, who will not submit to any other than God but also challenges God.

Evil is action

A famous *hadith qudsi* (sacred hadith) reflects how wrongdoing only is a sin. 'He who has intended a good deed and has not done it, God writes it down with himself as a full good deed, but if he has intended it and done it, God writes it down with himself as from ten good deeds to 700 times or many times. But if he has intended an evil deed and has not done it, God writes it down with himself as a good deed, but if he has intended it and done it, God writes it down as one evil deed. *Hadith* number 37, cited in Ibrahim and Johnson-Davies, *Forty Hadiths.*

For many poets, Satan becomes a tragic hero. In John Milton's (1608–74), *Paradise Lost*, Satan is a sophisticated character and orator, but is cut off from divine grace. For Rumi (1207–73), the two forces of good and evil exist only within man and it is up to man to make the right choices; there is no comic dualism. Yet while Satan/Iblis is a tempter, he is also a victim, a tragic hero, a spiritual guide and, above all, a true lover of God.

The condensed idea
Human freedom is a mixed blessing

19 Mi`raj

The *isra'* and *mi`raj* narratives – that is, the night journey and the ascension of Muhammad – are two of the most popular stories about the Prophet, alluded to in the Qur'an and embellished in Islamic devotional literature. The *mi`raj* of the Prophet is regarded as a foundational event in his life, when he ascendeded the heavens, met with previous prophets and learnt about worship and ritual prayer.

The *mi`raj* is alluded to in a specific Qur'anic verse, 'Glory be to God who took his servant by night from al-Masjid al-Haram to al-Masjid al-Aqsa, whose surroundings we have blessed, to show him of our signs' (Q17:1). The second set of verses refer to Muhammad being 'in the highest part of the horizon, then he approached and descended' (Q53:1-8). The vocabulary regarding this celestial ascension is vague and, although there is mention of a night journey – the *isra'* – the Qur'an makes no specific reference to the term *mi`raj*. The latter gained momentum in extra-Qur'anic material and went through a number of revisions in the course of the Middle Ages. The story is important for Muslims, not only because it weaves together history, theology and mystical biography, but because of its narrative on worship. It informs the Muslim about the number of obligatory ritual prayers and the importance of Muhammad's intercessionary role.

A HEAVENLY LADDER
The first part of this journey – the *isra'* – takes place when the angel Jibril (Gabriel) lifts the Prophet on to a heavenly mount called Buraq to accompany

TIMELINE

c. 621	624 CE	705 CE
Muhammad travels on his spiritual and physical Night Journey	Al-Aqsa becomes the *qibla,* or direction, for prayers	Al-Walid completes the al-Aqsa mosque

Muhammad on a journey from Mecca to Jerusalem. Once there, the Prophet leads the prayer with Abraham, Moses and Jesus on the Temple Mount. The second part is Muhammad's heavenly journey – described as climbing a heavenly ladder (*mi`raj*) – his ascension, in which he meets all the major prophets in the seven heavens, and that ends with Abraham right before the gates of paradise.

The ladder is described as coming down from the highest heaven, having alternate stairs of silver and gold, being encrusted with pearls and surrounded with angels on its right and left. There are stories relating to the prophets Muhammad meets, each of whom welcome him. When he sees Adam, he sees to Adam's right 'great dark masses and a gate exuding a fragrant smell, and to his left great dark masses and a gate exuding a foul, putrid smell'. Adam smiled when Muhammad looked right and wept when he looked left. Jibril tells Muhammad that on the right are the people of paradise while on the left are the people of hell. Muhammad himself becomes thirsty and Jibril offers him both a bowl of wine and one of milk. Even though celestial wine is permitted, when Muhammad chooses the milk, Jibril is pleased for this is the 'right way'.

> THE HEART DID NOT LIE ABOUT WHAT IT SAW, SO WILL YOU DISPUTE WITH HIM OVER WHAT HE SAW? HE SAW HIM AT A SECOND DESCENT, NEAR THE FARTHEST LOTE TREE.
> Q53:11–14

GOD'S PRESENCE

While there has been discussion as to whether this was a real physical journey of the body or a dream or a vision, another interpretation suggests that God himself accompanied 'his servant' on this journey. The event is alluded to in the Qur'an, when it is said that Muhammad reached the higher part of heaven, 'then he approached and descended, and was at a distance of two bow lengths or nearer, and he revealed to his servant what he revealed' (Q53:7–10). Later on, it is said that 'the sight [of the Prophet] did not swerve, nor did it turn away/transgress' (Q53:17). These verses, taken together, led to the creation of a vast body of literature that focused on

1035

Fatimid caliph al-Zahir builds the mosque that we see today

1967

Jerusalem comes under Israeli control

The five-times prayer

Ascension stories are about showing the hand of God in the lives of his prophets. In the case of the mi`raj, the story is richly infused with all kinds of symbolism. Central to the story are the apocalyptic and eschatological motifs that elevated the prophet to a new rank, regarding his possible physical and psychological proximity to God.

But one of the most famous stories connected with this journey relates to the fact that it was during the mi`raj that the five-times canonical prayers were established. The story is that God enjoined 50 prayers on Muhammad and his followers. As the Prophet was coming back down, he passed Moses, who wanted to know the number of prayers. When Muhammad replied that he had been ordered to pray 50 times per day, Moses was astonished and advised, 'Go back to your Lord and ask for a reduction'. Moses had more experience than Muhammad and was sure that his people would not be able to perform that many prayers. Muhammad accepted this advice out of reverence for Moses and went back to God asking for a reduction. The prayers were reduced to 40 but when Moses heard this, he sent Muhammad back to ask for a further reduction. This exchange continued until the number of obligatory prayers came to five. Even then Moses suggested a further reduction but the Prophet replied that he was now too ashamed to ask. Thus, the five daily prayers were established.

the Prophet's uniqueness among other prophets and, perhaps most significantly, whether he actually saw God. Some say that he saw God in his dream or that he saw only light. But one hadith, of which there are several variations, states that when the Prophet's wife Aisha was asked whether he had seen God during the mi`raj, she replied that this was a lie, that no one can see God, reciting the verse, 'Vision comprehends him not, but he comprehends all vision' (Q6:103).

THE MYSTICS' VIEW

However, for the mystics, the story reveals the Prophet's superior psychological strength in that he did not faint, but saw what he saw and stayed in the divine presence in full consciousness. The mi`raj also illustrates a particular distinction between the prophetic and the mystical journey explained so memorably in the fifth chapter of Muhammad Iqbal's seminal work, The Reconstruction of Religious Thought in Islam, in which the Sufi Abdul Quddus sighs longingly for Muhammad's experience. Muhammad's return to Earth is a sign of prophetic sobriety and responsibility, the recognition of an obligation to fulfil God's commands here on Earth. This contrasts with the words of those great Sufis who want to do away with everything that separates humankind from God in this life. Nowhere has this been expressed more hauntingly than in the words of the great Muslim saint Abdul Quddus of Gangoh: 'Muhammad of Arabia ascended the highest Heaven and returned. I swear by God that if I had reached that point, I should never have returned.'

Basing his desire to be with God on the narrative of Muhammad's ascension to heaven, this Sufi saint questions the Prophet's return. The mystic longs for that vision that the Prophet has already experienced. Unlike the prophetic role, which has no alternative but to return to Earth, the mystic has no such commitment, for his focus and goal are God alone. The Prophet has returned whereas the mystic would find any other experience now meaningless.

THE MI'RAJ IN ART

The *mi`raj* story captured the imagination of writers, poets and mystics, as well as that of ordinary Muslims. All kinds of fantastic and grandiose images as well as rhetorical devices have been used to portray this mysterious event. This event was celebrated in epic poetry and, by the 15th and 16th centuries, beautiful images depicting this narrative were found in Persian paintings.

A Persian painting depicting the Night Journey and Ascension of the Prophet

The condensed idea
The believer fears and desires a vision of God

20 Kalam

The term that comes closest to 'theology' in Islam is *kalam*, which means 'speech' or 'discussion'. Theological writing is usually the result of self-definition by a religious community. Emerging from the seventh century, the science of *kalam* became the science of discussing all things divine.

Kalam was a scholastic activity that tried to defend tenets of the faith and involved Muslims speaking to one another, as well as to those outside the faith, especially the Jews and the Christians. As interest in philosophy grew among Muslim thinkers under the Abbasid revolution of the 750s CE, *kalam* adopted the dialectic methodology of the Greeks and was influenced by Greek reasoning, logic and metaphysics.

SCHOOLS OF THEOLOGICAL THOUGHT

Many theological themes arose from religious and political issues faced by the early Muslim community, and included the relationship between free will and predestination, right belief, sin and salvation, the nature of ethical values, such as right and just, and the concept of the creation of the Qur'an. In addition, the whole epistemology of knowledge itself – divided broadly between divine knowledge and human knowledge – focused on the kind of knowledge God created in humankind.

Theologians could be broadly divided into rationalist and traditionalist. The rationalists were those who stressed the primacy of reason over revelation in case of any contradiction between the two. The traditionalists were those

TIMELINE

750s CE	8TH CENTURY CE
Clear influence of Greek reasoning, logic and philosophy upon Islamic thought	Appearance of the Mu`tazilite, rationalist school

thinkers who relied on the Qur'an, the *sunna* and the consensus of the scholars first and foremost as the basis of their theology.

By the eighth century, many questions had emerged, such as who was a true believer and whether only God knew the true state of a person's faith. One of the more significant discussions concerned the issue of free will. The Qadiriyya were a group who advocated that humankind had free will because God would not demand that mankind act virtuously if it did not have the freedom to do so. The Qadiriyya opposed the concept of predetermination of events by God (*qadar*). This also reflected their opposition to the ruling Umayyad caliphs, who justified their theological and political powers on the basis that God had ordained them.

> **THE HELL TO BE ENDURED HEREAFTER, OF WHICH THEOLOGY TELLS, IS NO WORSE THAN THE HELL WE MAKE FOR OURSELVES IN THIS WORLD BY HABITUALLY FASHIONING OUR CHARACTERS IN THE WRONG WAY.**
>
> William James (1842–1910)

Human free will to act was defended most vociferously by the more significant group called the Mu'tazila, known as the 'party of God's justice and unity'. The group appeared in the eighth century and its members often described as the rationalists of Islam who introduced Greek reasoning into Islamic theological discussions. By using modes of thought from Greek philosophy, they refined rational approaches to the interpretation of theological debate. They insisted that God had, in his justice, given humanity free will to act. Divine justice meant that God could not punish or reward humanity for actions that God himself had preordained. This also meant that human beings were responsible for their actions and could not attribute their wrongdoing to God.

THE CREATED QUR'AN

The Mu'tazila became most prominent for their doctrine of the 'created Qur'an'. Until then, the orthodox position was that the Qur'an, as 'the word of God', was coeternal with God and uncreated. The Qur'an was God's speech in

833 CE

The Mu'tazilite inquisition (*minha*): persecution of those opposing the 'createdness' of the Qur'an

935 CE

Birth of al-Ashari; middle way between scripture and reason

Human freedom

One of the most systematic attempts to defend God's omnipotence and attribute moral responsibility to humankind is found in the famous letter of Hasan al-Basri (642–728 CE) to the caliph Abd al-Malik. Whether or not he actually wrote this letter, it is a defence of the theory of predestination. Throughout the letter, Hasan's aim is to reconcile God's determinism with the moral and religious freedom of human beings. God does not wrong man and since God had created man to worship him, he would not therefore predetermine disobedience and then punish man. The evidence for this defence is taken from revelation itself and Hasan argues two fundamental principles: namely, that God has created humanity to worship him and that evil does not come from God.

the literal sense. Instead, the Mu`tazila championed the doctrine that the Qur'an had been created 'in time' and that it was not coeternal with God, since this would compromise God's unity. This doctrine was given official decree by the caliph al-Ma`mun (786–833 CE), who declared it binding on all Muslims. Anyone who opposed the doctrine risked the death penalty, a period known as the 'inquisition' (*mihna*). For the Mu`tazila, God's unity was the ultimate defence for many of their doctrines, which included a metaphorical understanding of the anthropomorphic verses in the Qur'an. So when the Qur'an says 'God's face' or 'God's hands' or 'God sits', this did not mean any human form could be applied to God; God was completely transcendent and other and eternal.

One of the most significant figures of the time, opposing the doctrine of the created Qur'an and advocating a literal understanding of the anthropomorphic verses, was Ahmad Ibn Hanbal (780–855 CE). Some claim he introduced the doctrine of *bila kayfa* (without [asking] how) – in other words, that believers should not question issues of which they could only ever have a limited understanding, and that faith was in accepting certain paradoxes without asking how. While Ahmad Ibn Hanbal was imprisoned several times for his views, which went against the official doctrines of the state, the doctrines of the Mu`tazila proved unpopular and were abolished as state doctrine, under Caliph al-Mutawakkil in 850 CE.

The person generally credited with founding a middle way between scripturalism and rationalism is al-Ash`ari (d. *c.* 935 CE). Originally a follower of the Mu`tazila school, he changed to the more traditional Sunni views on God's complete omnipotence and predestination. On the issue of the anthropomorphic Qur'anic verses, he argued for a literal understanding and, according to some, is also credited with having the doctrine of *bila kayfa*. On the issue of predestination, al-Ash`ari argued that God is the only creator of human actions and, while he creates everything, human beings 'acquire' them in time and so assume responsibility for their actions. Al-Ash`ari is credited with writing a Sunni creed in which belief in God, his angels, his books and messengers, came to define mainstream Sunni Islam.

Doing good

The British Lebanese historian Albert Hourani (1915–93) argued that Ash`arite thinking had prevailed in Sunni Islam, by which human acts are right only when God commands man or recommends to him to do them. In an essay entitled 'Ethical Presuppositions of the Qur'an', he suggested that human intelligence can discern and cultivate moral goodness. Hourani's dilemma was that the Qur'an couples so closely two qualities of the good person: belief in God and doing right. The phrase 'those who believe and do right acts' is constant. Thus the question is, do only those who believe, do right acts.? And when do people believe is it their faith that causes them to do good or their own sense of moral discernment?

PHILOSOPHICAL THOUGHT

Philosophy also developed under the Abbasids, via translations of Greek philosophy and science, so retaining its non-Islamic origins. Abbasid rule witnessed the appearance of distinguished Islamic philosophers, such as al-Kindi (d. *c.* 870 CE), al-Farabi (d. 950 CE) and Ibn Sina (d. 1037), who claimed a rightful stake in knowledge of the divine and went on to become leading intellects of the philosophical world. Yet it is reasonable to conclude that neither speculative theology nor philosophy could challenge the centrality of Islamic law as the major intellectual enterprise of the Islamic world.

The condensed idea
The Qur'an is first a book of guidance

21 Kafir

The word *kufr* is usually translated as denial or unbelief, with '*kafir*' (pl. *kafirun*) the most common Islamic term for 'disbeliever' or 'unbeliever'. The distinction between believers and unbelievers is central to the Qur'an.

A central message of the Qur'an is that of calling people to believe. Believers and unbelievers are often placed in contrasting imagery. The Qur'an consistently couples its praise of believers with a clear and consistent condemnation of unbelievers, who are described as arrogant, blind and stubborn for their failure to follow Muhammad's message. The break between Muhammad and the unbelievers is most clearly expressed in chapter 109 of the Qur'an, called The Unbelievers (*surah al-kafirun*):

> Say (Muhammad): 'O Unbelievers!
> I do not worship what you worship,
> Nor are you worshippers of what I worship,
> Nor am I a worshipper of what you worship,
> Nor are you worshippers of what I worship,
> To you, your religion and to me, mine.' (Q109:1–6)

A LACK OF GRATITUDE

Reading *kufr* solely as 'unbelief' masks some of the nuance of the term in the Qur'an, however. Across many Qur'anic verses *kufr* is used primarily as the opposite of *shukr*, meaning 'gratitude'. The Qur'an

TIMELINE

622–719 CE	14TH CENTURY
Khawarij and their radical position on *takfir*	Ibn Kathir's *Tafsir* defines eight kinds of major unbeliefs

repeatedly explains how all aspects of man's life are a gift and favour from God,

> And God has extracted you from the wombs of your mothers not knowing a thing, and he made for you intellect and hearing and vision that perhaps you would be grateful. (Q16:78)

Thus, in the Qu'ranic perspective, the religious life is primarily one of gratitude to God for the countless gifts we receive. This depicts the unbeliever as someone who, above all, is ungrateful to God. Unbelievers take God's gifts and yet reject God, failing to thank him,

> And He gave you from all you asked of Him. And if you should count the favours of God, you could not enumerate them. Indeed, mankind is most unjust and ungrateful. (Q14:34)

THE BELIEF OF SINNERS

In the later development of Islamic law and theology, the sense of *kufr* as ingratitude receded, and the term gradually came to be understood as unbelief. What specifically constitutes 'unbelief' became a key issue in early intra-Muslim debate, however. The relationship between faith and acts – primarily the question as to whether the Muslim who commits sinful acts remains a believer – was a central discussion during the early centuries of Islam. Muslims responded to this in a variety of ways. The most infamous response was that of the early Kharijite school, who held that the Muslim who sins, but does not repent becomes an unbeliever. This reading of apostasy saw the Kharijites become notorious for their killing of other Muslims whom they considered to have left the faith, including the Prophet's cousin and son-in-law, Ali. Today, the Kharijite label remains a

IF THE ONLY PRAYER YOU SAID WAS THANK YOU THAT WOULD BE ENOUGH.
Meister Eckhart

1893-1987	20TH CENTURY
Al-Hilali claims *kafir* is one who disbelieves any of the articles of faith	*Kafir* used increasingly to describe anyone who is not a Muslim; Spanish *cafre* means 'uncouth' or 'savage'

Friendship and belief

In the Quran, friendship and social ties are envisaged largely within the theme of forging alliances. These alliances can be on the human plane between individuals, politically between communities or between human beings and God.

In the first context, the Qur'an's reference to friends includes those whom the fledgling Muslim community looks to as becoming allies of the new faith. The Qur'an repeatedly advises against forming bonds of protection or alliance with those who are not from the new category of believers. The Qur'an also stresses the wrongs of making alliances with those who ridicule the Prophet's message, 'O you who believe, do not take as allies (friends) those who ridicule your religion and make fun of it, whether people who were given the scripture before you, or believers, and be mindful of God if you are true believers' (Q5:57).

The Qur'an speaks of friendship with God, where God is a helper and a friend, 'Your friends are God and his messenger and those who believe, who establish prayer, give zakat and bow down in worship' (Q5:55). Some interpret these verses to mean that Muslims should only be friends with other Muslims.

But such rigorist conceptions of piety are challenged by pluralist societies in which there are people of all faiths and none share the same space and commitment to social harmony and peace. In multicultural societies, religion alone cannot be upheld as the defining premise of any friendship. Those we choose as friends says something about who we are as people.

common motif and is often levelled against contemporary radical groups for their anathematizing of other Muslims.

Mainstream Islamic theology sought to distinguish between major and minor forms of *kufr*. Major *kufr* involved acts that placed one outside the fold of Islam, such as rejecting the prophecy of Muhammad or the authority of the Qur'an. Minor *kufr* related to sinful acts that did not lead to excommunication, such as missing prayers or drinking intoxicants.

PEOPLE OF THE BOOK

In terms of locating *kufr* outside the boundaries of Islam, the People of the Book – the Qur'anic title for Jews and Christians – have occupied an ambivalent position in Islamic thought as both believers *and* unbelievers. Jews and Christians reject Muhammad's prophecy and the authority of the Qur'an, and are accused of having altered their religion. Yet these communities also follow revealed scripture and worship the same God (Q29:46). In the development of Islamic law this peculiar form of Jewish and Christian unbelief was enshrined in the *dhimmi* system. *Dhimmi* translates as 'protected' and denotes how, as fellow scriptuaries, Jews and Christians remain free to practice their religion under classical Islamic law. In exchange, they were to pay a poll tax, known as the *jizya*, and were subject to other social restrictions.

KUFR AND ISLAMISM

For many Muslims today, the concept of *kufr* has lost the theological and legal complexities discussed above. Increasingly, many treat *kufr* as a blanket term that demarcates all aspects of non-Muslim religion or culture. In this sense *kufr* serves as a 'boundary reinforcer': a broad social label that serves to strengthen Muslim identity. Particularly within Islamist trends, one finds matters as diverse as democracy, music and even other forms of Islam, such as Shi`ism or Sufism, invariably consumed under the broad category of *kufr* (see Chapter 48).

The frequent use of *kafir* and the popular derogatory *kuffar* by jihadists and militant groups, has brought these terms to Western consciousness in dramatic ways. The historical binary between the Dar al-Islam (House of Islam) versus the Dar al-Harb (House of War) has mutated into the House of the *Kuffar*, in which the whole of the West is targeted as a land of unbelievers, in ideological opposition to Islam.

This popular, but derogatory, use of the term masks the often complex theological and legal classical discussions over what specifically constitutes belief and unbelief. Popular Muslim understandings of *kufr* today are also often very far from the origins of the concept in the Qur'an – where it is primarily an ungrateful rejection in the eyes of God for the countless divine blessings we continue to receive.

The condensed idea
Belief is gratitude to God

22 Prayer

The relationship between faith and rituals is a paradox. To the outsider, ritual is the most obvious sign of the character of a religion and the identity of its believers. Yet ritual can never quite capture faith, for faith transcends form and imagery. In Islam, the most central ritual is prayer, observed in the five-times-daily prayers called *salat*. Many might say that, in turning to God in any kind of prayer, human beings experience a little taste of eternity.

In Islam, the word that comes closest to any sense of ritual is *ibada*, which actually means 'worship'. However, *ibada* can refer to a whole range of acts for conforming life to God's will. Alongside prayer (*salat*), the witness to faith (*shahada*; see Chapter 10), almsgiving (*zakat*; see Chapter 24), pilgrimage (*hajj*; see Chapter 25) and fasting during Ramadan (*sawm*; see Chapter 23) are generally understood to constitute the 'five pillars of Islam'. Anyone who embarks on an introductory course on Islam in a Western university will be taught that these pillars are the central feature of Muslim life and piety. The Qur'an does not refer to any sense of foundational pillars, though it does repeatedly refer to the importance of observing prayer and almsgiving as righteous activities. Instead, the idea of Islam being founded on five pillars rests on a saying of the Prophet:

> Islam has been built on five [pillars] testifying that there is no god but God and that Muhammad is the messenger of Allah, performing the prayers, paying the alms, making the pilgrimage to the House and fasting in Ramadan.

TIMELINE

5,000 YEARS AGO	5TH CENTURY CE	838–932 CE
Acts of prayer attested	Origins of the 'Jesus Prayer'	Al-Tabari allows women to lead men in prayer

THE CALL TO PRAYER

The Qur'an exhorts Muslims to pray, 'be steadfast in prayer' (Q2:43). Anyone who has visited a Muslim country will be aware of the five-times call to prayer – the *adhan*. The muezzin calls the faithful to prayer because this formal prayer is a constant reminder to the believer to make time and space for remembering God. The message in this call is that God is great and that prayer is a route to individual prosperity and salvation. Prayer is also used by some Muslims as an indication of individual devotion, in particular, the observance of early morning or daybreak prayer known as *fajr*.

> WHEN THERE IS NO SHOULDER TO CRY ON, THERE IS THE FLOOR, CRY IN PROSTRATION TO THE LORD AND YOUR PROBLEMS WILL GO AWAY.
>
> Unknown

The basic unit of *salat* consists of a cycle called *rak'a* and each *salat* has a special number of cycles. The other times for *salat* are noon (*zuhr*), mid-afternoon (*asr*), sunset (*maghrib*) and evening (*isha*). While the Qur'an speaks of prayer several times, it does not explicitly formulate formal five-times prayer. According to Muslim tradition, the number five became fixed following instructions given to Muhammad during his heavenly journey (*mi`raj*; see Chapter 19).

The Qur'an does however refer to several rituals associated with prayer – performing ablutions before prayer (*wudu*), bowing, prostrating and facing in a set direction called the *qibla*. Ritual purity is a requirement to formal prayer and for this reason, women do not observe *salat* during menstruation or during the post-partum bleeding. The Qur'an singles out Friday prayers, in which the implication is that believers should congregate in prayer:

> O you who have believed, when [the *adhan*] is called for the prayer on the day of Jumu'ah [Friday], then proceed to the remembrance of Allah and leave trade. That is better for you, if you only knew. (Q62:9)

1820

Female imams in female-only mosques in China

2014

First Muslim prayer service at Washington National Cathedral; Muslim prayers held at the Vatican

Prayer broadcasts

In July 2015, German TV broadcast live Muslim Eid prayers from a mosque in a town near Munich. This was the first time this had happened in the country's history. The prayers were aired from the Penzberg Mosque on public television and radio broadcaster Bayerischen Rundfunk. The sermon marked the beginning of the Eid el-Fitr holiday and the end of the fasting month of Ramadan. Germany is believed to have nearly four million Muslims and more than 200,000 of the asylum seekers, who arrived in 2014, came from African and Middle Eastern countries. This rise in asylum applications has been met with a growing trend of xenophobic attacks targeting non-European migrants. The broadcast, which included Qur'an recitations and speeches from Catholic and Protestant priests, is a step towards achieving greater harmony in German society and more mutual understanding.

Friday prayers are accompanied by a sermon called a *khutbah*. Muslims can pray in a congregation in a mosque, at home on their own or with their family. In a congregation, people stand behind an imam, who is not a priest but simply someone entrusted to lead the prayer. Sections of the Qur'an are often recited as part of prayers. A portable prayer rug is used at all times, especially if clean space is unavailable. Imams are traditionally men, the understanding being that a woman can only lead an all-female congregation.

Prayer is mentioned in the Qur'an as one of the most righteous activities and is often paired with almsgiving as intrinsic to a righteous life:

The believing men and believing women are helpers of one another. They enjoin what is right and forbid what is wrong and establish prayer and give *zakat* and obey God and his messenger. Those – God will have mercy upon them. (Q9:71)

VOLUNTARY PRAYER

During the two Eid celebrations, Muslims attend the mosque to perform prayers that are recommended, but not obligatory. There are also many non-compulsory prayers, including as a nighttime prayer called *witr*. Praying during the night requires extra discipline and there are many traditions stating that true piety is reflected in such prayer. The most common of all non-ritualized prayers is the *du`a*, an individual's personal prayer to God. These can be said at any time and anywhere. They are a personal supplication, reminding the believer that the transcendent and the paradisal are never far away. The most common phrases of prayer are 'God is great' or 'Glory be to God'. These are also used by Muslims in conversation. Prayer provides daily structure, rhythmic form and remembrance of God. Above all it provides a way of directly communicating with God in fear, in gratitude and in hope.

THE LIVES OF SAINTS

While hagiographical literature may be given to pious exaggeration, it does reveal a particular aspect of intense spirituality. Prayer was the ultimate refuge, and for women Sufis, the worship of God could not be compromised with domestic duties. For example, Rabi`a bint Isma`il could not love her husband with marital love and told him that she prayed constantly because she could not hear the call to prayer without thinking of Judgement Day. There are many accounts of men and women who engaged in all-night vigils, fasting and praying, prepared to die at any moment.

Optional prayers

Prostration is such an intrinsic part of Muslim prayer that there are many prayers that are not obligatory but offer the opportunity for Muslims to prostrate in humility to God. A *nafl* prayer is a supererogatory prayer – that is, it is optional but considered a pious exercise. *Nafl* prayers can be performed as many times as one wishes and are seen as drawing one closer to God. *Tarawih* prayers refer to extra prayers performed by Sunni Muslims during the nights of Ramadan. While these are also optional, many Muslims return to the mosques at night during this month to pray *tarawih* as an act of devotion.

The condensed idea
Prayer is remembrance of God

23 Ramadan and fasting

Fasting during the ninth lunar month of Ramadan is one of the best-known of the prescribed practices in Islam and the fourth pillar of Islam. The Arabic term for 'fasting' is *sawm*. The practice is outwardly reflected in an abstention from food or drink between the hours of sunrise and sunset. Fasting comes to an end with the Eid al-Fitr (the canonical feast of fast-breaking) at the end of the month.

The Qur'an prescribes fasting for the new community just as fasting had been prescribed for those that became before – that is, the Jews and the Christians. However, fasting in Ramadan is made distinct by its length and time. The importance of the month of Ramadan is not just in fasting. This is also the month in which the 'Qur'an was sent down, a clear guidance for humankind':

> The month of Ramadan [is that] in which was revealed the Qur'an,
> a guidance for the people and clear proofs of guidance and criterion.
> So whoever sights [the new moon of] the month, let him fast it; and
> whoever is ill or on a journey – then an equal number of other days.
> Allah intends for you ease and does not intend for you hardship and
> [wants] for you to complete the period and to glorify Allah for that [to]
> which He has guided you; and perhaps you will be grateful (Q2:185).

The Muslim who is fasting should also abstain from sexual relations during these hours and anything else that might lead to breaking the

TIMELINE

610 CE	624 CE
Qur'an first revealed to Muhammad during month of Ramadan	Fasting during Ramadan revealed

fast. A fast that is broken unintentionally is forgiven and remains a fast, but there are various forms of expiation for intentionally breaking the fast. Categories of people who are exempt from fasting include women during menstruation, pregnancy or immediately after childbirth, travellers, the infirm and the sick. Although most Muslim families encourage young children to keep some of the fasts, it is not a requirement and there should be no coercion.

RELIGIOUS REFLECTION

The paradox of Ramadan is that, although fasting can be difficult, and a genuine test for many, the month itself is a month of celebration and joy, for this is when the Qur'an was revealed.

> HE LEAVES HIS FOOD, DRINK AND DESIRES FOR MY SAKE. HIS FASTING IS FOR ME . . . I WILL GIVE THE REWARD FOR IT, AND FOR EVERY GOOD DEED, HE WILL RECEIVE TEN SIMILAR TO IT.
>
> *Hadith* in Bukhari

Both day and night are sacred times for a heightened worship and increased gratitude for the blessings in one's life. In Muslim countries, working hours are modified to accommodate fasting requirements in order to enable those fasting to continue working. People often slow down daily activities to devote more time to religious reflection and many will go on a spiritual retreat (*i`itikaf*), which involves spending day and night in prayer and worship in a local mosque. Very often mosques have nightly readings of the Qur'an, which result in a complete recitation of the Qur'an over 30 days. Many Muslims attend mosques more regularly during Ramadan and perform a special prayer called *tarawih*, which is voluntary, not obligatory. When it is time to break the fast at sunset, for *maghrib* prayers, families often meet and share food. This evening meal is known as *iftar*. The Prophet is said to have broken his fast with two dates and water before praying, so most Muslims continue to open their meal with dates.

It is difficult for the non-Muslim to recognize these aspects of Ramadan, as the whole ritual is largely equated with self-denial as a means of

1966
Pope Paul VI changes strictly regulated Roman Catholic fasting requirements

2014
Fasting in Iceland and Norway 22 hours long due to timing of Ramadan

Fasting and sport

Fasting demands both mental and physical stamina. For most Muslims, it means an interruption of their daily lives for a while, until they become accustomed to the demands of fasting, especially during the long fasts of the summer months.

But for sportsmen and women, the fasts can be far more challenging. In 2012, the London Olympics fell in the month of Ramadan. As top athletes can lose up to 15 per cent of their body weight in sweat as they practice, many religious leaders in Egypt, Algeria, Saudi Arabia and the UAE exempted their athletes from fasting. The Egyptian al-Azhar University gave a response that included travel and extreme hardship as reasons for exempting the athletes that particular year. The Grand Mufti of Dubai determined that the athletes could make up their missed fasts when they returned, and Algeria gave similar reasons, adding that the athletes were travelling in the service of their country.

However, some athletes did fast, including Suleiman Nyambui of Tanzania, who took silver in the 5,000 metres at the 1980 Summer Olympics. Many British Muslims saw these exemptions as part of the flexibility of Islam that allows for reasonable accommodation of individual needs and contexts.

self-purification. Fasting during Ramadan is not about giving up one kind of food or drink; it is about not eating or drinking anything during the prescribed period.

ACCOMMODATING THE FAST

Because Muslims observe the lunar calendar, fasting moves through the seasons, occurring some 11 days earlier each year. In recent years, many Muslims have questioned whether the practice of fasting can be changed during long summer months, when the sun sets very late.

Similarly, new legal guidelines have emerged for those Muslims living in the two polar regions, where there is either continuous daylight or continuous darkness for some months. Furthermore, as more and more Muslims settle in the West, how can they reconcile the demands of fasting with the responsibilities of the workplace – can there be some form of concession or exemption? These are difficult challenges that have been met with a wide variety of humane responses to ease the demands of fasting in these countries. For example, some religious scholars advocate observing fasting hours according to the closest Muslim country or, if a person cannot fast for long hours, that they make up the fast when it becomes easier. However, there is no consensus on these issues and Muslims often follow the recommendations or practices of their local mosques or communities.

VOLUNTARY FASTS

While fasting during Ramadan is obligatory, there are also voluntary fasts one can keep. Voluntary fasting is recommended on the day of Ashura, the tenth day of the month of Muharram. Fasting, however, also has a certain redemptive effect so that one can keep a fast or several fasts as an act of atonement or penance (*kaffara*) for any transgressions or sins. The Qur'an itself mentions several occasions on which one should observe an atoning fast alongside other atoning recommendations, such as freeing a slave or seeking repentance.

Many of the Prophetic *hadiths* refer to fasting as a ritual most precious to God. This is because fasting is difficult: it requires discipline and it is done primarily for love of God. According to Bukhari:

> The Prophet said, 'By him in whose hands my soul is, the smell coming out from the mouth of a fasting person is better in the sight of Allah than the smell of musk. [Allah says about the fasting person], "He has left his food, drink and desires for my sake. The fast is for me. So I will reward (the fasting person) for it and the reward of good deeds is multiplied ten times".'

The condensed idea
Most religions encourage some form of fasting

24 Almsgiving

Zakat, commonly translated as 'almsgiving' or 'alms tax', is the third pillar of Islam. Prayer and *zakat* are frequently mentioned in the Qur'an as the two principal obligations in Islam. *Zakat* is not meant to be a solitary act, given in some void from one believer to another; it was always seen as the concrete expression of faith (*iman*) to help the poor and needy, and to contribute to social justice in the Muslim community.

The noun *zakat* appears 32 times in the Qur'an, often placed immediately after ritual prayer in terms of the believer's duties:

Righteousness is not that you turn your faces towards the East or the West, but [true] righteousness is [in] one who believes in God, the Last Day, the angels, the Book, and the prophets and gives wealth, in spite of love for it, to relatives, orphans, the needy, the traveller, those who ask [for help] and for freeing slaves; [and who] establishes prayer and gives zakat; [those who] fulfill their promise when they promise; and [those who] are patient in poverty and hardship and during battle. Those are the ones who have been truthful and God fearing (2:177).

Giving to the poor and the traveller is a repeated Qur'anic command. While the Qur'an exhorts Muslims to spend some of their wealth on the needy, the precise details concerning donation and payment were worked out over a period of time by the legal schools. This included discussions about who collected *zakat*, which crops, animals and other goods were liable for

TIMELINE

632 CE	717–20 CE
Abu Bakr institutes statutory *zakat* system	During the reign of Umar, it is reported that no one in Medina needed *zakat*

zakat and other political and social realities. A common understanding is that *zakat* should be paid at 2.5 per cent on wealth, such as gold, silver and merchandise held after one year.

PURIFING YOUR WEALTH

While giving to various categories of people is a repeated theme in the Qur'an, the work remains silent on the details of poverty and need, and also on the question as to who, exactly, the poor are; the dominant command is simply to give.

> **NO ONE HAS EVER BECOME POOR BY GIVING.**
> Anne Frank,
> *Diary of Anne Frank*

Zakat is not charity; it is like a debt one owes to those who deserve it. The Islamic imperative, to give to the poor and the needy in various ways, is based on the idea that, while wealth divides humankind into rich and poor, it is only through consideration of the poor and the needy that the rich 'purify' their wealth.

Wealth accumulation is not in itself a sin, for wealth is simply matter, and matter should be seen as morally neutral. In the same way, imposed poverty is not a virtue. However, wealth can be enslaving and simply *having* material fortune contributes to a morally inert life. Thus, the notion of purity is contained in the word *zakat* – by giving from one's wealth to the poor and needy or for the general welfare of society, one's remaining wealth is purified and lawful for use.

CHARITY AND OSTENTATION

The ethics of purifying the wealth one has through just distribution is a major theme in Islamic thought. While *zakat* is seen as obligatory, the word *sadaqa* implies voluntary giving and is often translated as charity. Despite this distinction, the words are frequently used interchangeably. What they share is the imperative to give and to do good.

2012
Islamic financial analysts estimate *zakat* spending exceeds US$200 billion per year.

2014
Study states that widespread poverty persists in Islamic world despite *zakat* collections every year.

Charity and generosity are applauded and encouraged, but ostentation is to be avoided, for ostentation – however little – annuls good deeds. Nor should generosity ever become wastefulness. The excess of lavishness is also seen as a moral defect. The believer is encouraged to 'spend in the way of God', but this spending must be kept in balance.

There is, in Islamic thought, a constant reminder that wealth is to be shared but this sharing must exist alongside prudence. Yet, as a general theme, there is quite clearly a preference for spending one's wealth, on oneself but especially on others. There is an account from the life of the Prophet, who, it is said, gave so generously – even to those who were rude – that one recipient of his generosity urged his countrymen to become Muslims, 'for Muhammad gives like one who has no fear of poverty'. Many of the great saints spoke of limitless generosity, claiming that the truly faithful – those ones who are close to God – keep nothing for themselves, neither the reputation of being good nor the hope of a reward in the hereafter.

It should be noted that, while giving to the poor and the traveller is a repeated Qur'anic command, so a Muslim's duties to look after relatives. In fact relatives, especially if they are poor, must be a priority when giving away wealth:

> The Prophet said, 'if someone has poor relatives and instead of spending on them he gives charity to others, his charity will not be accepted by Allah, and Allah will not look at him on the Day of Resurrection. However, if he himself is poor, he should keep ties with them by visiting them and keeping informed of their situation'.

CONSCIENCE AND A JUST SOCIETY

Over the years, the collection of *zakat* has become increasingly difficult and the payment of *zakat* is now usually a matter of the individual's conscience. In some Muslim countries, government bureaucracy assumes responsibility for collection from the individual. But many Muslims donate to various organizations as a way of making their contribution to society.

Zakat as solidarity

While the payment of *zakat* is obligatory for adult Muslims, the actual practice of *zakat* in terms of donations, collections and redistribution of wealth varies significantly over time and space.

Muslim legal schools of the medieval period debated whether *zakat* was owed to the ruler to distribute or, if the ruler was unjust, whether it could be given by one individual to another. Today, the payment of *zakat* can be construed as an act of pious solidarity among Muslims that traverses nation states. Nations states that have insisted on the state collection of *zakat* or a centralized *zakat* system, such as Pakistan and Malaysia, have found these practices to be unpopular.

Globalization and the growth of mass media means that, whenever there is a natural disaster, relief agencies arrive with money and other forms of material needs. When Muslim countries are hit by a natural disaster, *zakat* is often donated as a trans-Islamic imperative. Consider the floods in Pakistan in 2010. The Organization of the Islamic Conference (OIC) urged Muslims, regardless of their nationality or residency, to give their *zakat* to Pakistan. This appeal was backed by the International Fiqh Committee approving an individual's choice to pay *zakat* to those who were more in need. This has led some to claim that many Muslims see their payment of *zakat* to Muslims first rather than anyone who is deserving, as an act of transnational solidarity.

Zakat remains an obligation, the purpose of which is to create a more charitable and socially just society. But *zakat* is not simply about material wealth, it is also about an attitude to others. It serves as a moral compass in the inner life of the Muslim.

It is said that the first deed that should accompany faith is charity. If one does not have anything material to give, or is too weak to help someone else, the very least a person can do as a charitable act is restrain himself from harming others.

The condensed idea
Paying *zakat* purifies your wealth

25 The hajj

Each year, Mecca attracts several million Muslims from all over the world, who perform the great pilgrimage, or *hajj*, the fifth pillar of Islam. For many Muslims, this is the defining ritual of their lives, the ultimate visual expression of the unity of all believers and their equality in the eyes of God.

The requirement to perform the *hajj* is stated in the Qur'an: 'Pilgrimage to the House [of God] is a duty owed to God by people who are able to undertake it' (Q3:97). Muslims, both men and women, should perform the pilgrimage at least once in their lifetime if they are physically and financially able to do so. Many Muslims perform more than one *hajj*, sometimes dedicating a pilgrimage to deceased parents or other loved ones.

THE INFLUENCE OF ABRAHAM

Pilgrimage to sacred sites occurs in most religious traditions, and pilgrimage to Mecca existed before Islam. However, it was transformed with the advent of Islam, which gave the pilgrimage new spiritual and symbolic value. The core of the *hajj* is based on a particular Abrahamic story in which Abraham's wife, Hagar and her son Isma`il (Ishmael), are the central characters, around whom many of the rituals are based. In the Islamic narrative, God tells Abraham to take Hagar and their son Isma`il to Arabia in order to escape the jealousy of Abraham's first wife, Sarah. Hagar is left alone in the Arabian desert, and her son begins to get thirsty and cries for water. In her desperation, Hagar runs seven times between the hills of Safa and Marwa, outside Mecca, where finally water appears miraculously

TIMELINE

2000 BCE	630 CE
Elements of *hajj* can be traced back to Abraham	Muhammad enters Mecca and cleanses Kaaba by destroying all the pagan idols

in the well of *zamzam*, a point at which the angel Jibril (Gabriel) is said to have struck the ground. The running of Hagar between the hills has since become a ritual of the *hajj*.

THE HAJJ EVENT

The *hajj* to Mecca and the surrounding areas is an annual ritual lasting up to seven days. It takes place in the first half of the last month of the year, known as Dhu'l-Hijja. On the seventh day of the month, pilgrims in a state of ritual purity (*ihram*) make a statement of intent to perform the *hajj*. Men put on a special garment – two seamless unsewn pieces of cloth. In wearing these simple clothes, all worshippers appear the same and any distinction of race, wealth or background disappear in this sacred place. Women must be covered except for their faces. As part of the intention to perform the *hajj*, pilgrims recite the words 'At your service O God, at your service'.

> **RELIGION POINTS TO THAT AREA OF HUMAN EXPERIENCE WHERE, IN ONE WAY OR ANOTHER, MAN COMES UPON MYSTERY AS A SUMMONS TO PILGRIMAGE.**
> Frederick Buechner (b. 1926)

The first rite is circumambulation (*tawaf*) of the Kaaba, seven times in an anticlockwise direction. Then, following the kissing, touching or gesturing towards the Black Stone set in the eastern wall of the Kaaba, the pilgrims run seven times between the two small hills of Safa and Marwa, and prayers are said around the Kaaba.

On the eighth day, the pilgrimage proper begins. The pilgrims assemble in Mina just outside Mecca and stay there for one night. The next morning they make the visit to the plains of Arafat, where they assemble on the Mount of Mercy from where Muhammad is said to have delivered his last sermon. The gathering at Arafat is symbolic of the gathering of all of humanity on the Day of Judgement. The pilgrims perform prayers. They ask for mercy and many remain standing as they pray from noon

632 CE

Muhammad performs pilgrimage with large number of followers; instructs on the rites of *hajj*

2015

Over two million pilgrims at the *hajj* in Mecca; stampede kills over 600 people.

till sunset, a rite known as 'standing in front of God' (*wuquf*). Towards the end of the day the pilgrims depart for Muzdalifah, a valley between Arafat and Mina, where they combine the two prayers of *maghrib* and *isha*. Many pilgrims sleep under the open sky and, on this night, they also collect small pebbles.

On the tenth day, after returning from Muzdalifah, the pilgrims spend the night at Mina. Here they throw the pebbles at the three granite pillars that commemorate the place at which Abraham threw stones at Satan. After the stone throwing, animals such as sheep, goats or camels are slaughtered in a ritual known as the *Eid al-Adha*: 'the festival of the sacrifice'. This day is celebrated by Muslims all over the world, who slaughter animals in abattoirs for personal consumption or to send to the poor. After sacrificing an animal, male pilgrims either shave or trim their hair and women cut a small lock of theirs. On the same, or the following day, the pilgrims revisit the mosque in Mecca for another circumambulation and they walk between the two hills of Safa and Marwa. While not necessary, many pilgrims also travel to Medina to pay respect to the Prophet's tomb in the Prophet's mosque.

During the *hajj*, pilgrims should refrain from sexual activity or any adornment, including shaving and wearing perfume. The *hajj* is not an easy ritual for everyone, but is seen as a defining journey of sacrifice, patience and self transformation.

HAJJ TRENDS

In the past, *hajj* was a ritual often performed in the later years of one's life but it has increased in popularity among the young. Muslims usually go on the *hajj* in groups and increasingly travel by means of *hajj* packages, which are offered by many airlines and travel agents. For the Saudi authorities, the logistical challenges of *hajj* grow every year with the number of pilgrims rising (see also, Chapter 6). Such huge numbers means that, tragically,

15th-century attestation certificate for a *hajj* performed by Maymanah, daughter of Muhammad al-Zardili.

there are always accidents or deaths. However, modern transport, better sanitation and increased housing mean that, for most people, the *hajj* can be performed with relative ease. It remains the most dramatic and spiritual of Islamic rituals.

Hajj or marriage

An interesting, but curious phenomenon among Western Muslims is that more and more newly married or young couples are choosing to go on *hajj* early on in their lives. Whereas a generation ago, many people performed *hajj* in their later years – or even in old age – this new trend shows how religious priorities and sense of individual piety can change over time.

Among the issues discussed in classical legal sources is whether priority should be given to marriage or *hajj* for young men. The answers are mixed for various reasons. Firstly, marriage is not compulsory, whereas *hajj* is a legal obligation for those who can afford it. However, if a man finds it difficult to remain single and chaste, then he should give priority to marriage. Marriage is often compared to necessities like food and drink. If a man does not have enough money to get married but wishes to do so, some jurists argue that he can be given money from *zakat* funds to help him. Delay in marriage is not considered beneficial.

Modern jurists generally agree that it is better to delay the *hajj* and be married first. It would seem that the contemporary trend towards getting married and then performing *hajj* very soon after, is seen by some as a double act of piety.

The condensed idea
The purpose of *hajj* is spiritual transformation

26 Hospitality

In Islam, hospitality is a virtue that lies at the very basis of the Islamic ethical system. It is a concept rooted in the pre-Islamic Bedouin virtues of welcome and generosity within the harsh desert environment. The concept can be found in the Arabic root *diyāfa*. The Prophet is reported to have said, 'There is no good in the one who is not hospitable'.

At its most basic level, hospitality is regarded as a virtue in all three monotheistic religions and has long been a central feature of Islamic cultures, with precedents rooted in both Byzantine and Sasanian traditions. The Latin forms, *hospes* and *hospitis* denote host, guest or stranger, while *hostis* can suggest stranger as friend or foe. Whereas the stranger was seen as a problem in classical antiquity and in the biblical Near East – and thus occupied a large niche in legal works – in Islamic thought, discussions on hospitality focus largely on the host/guest relationship and host/traveller, rather than that of host/stranger. Indeed despite strangers being everywhere, the word for stranger (*ajnabi*) is absent from the Qur'an.

PLAYING HOST

Hosting the guest, or welcoming the stranger, is a central event in the world's great wisdom traditions. Many state that the stranger embodies the presence of God and brings blessings in multiple ways. This theme is most strikingly present in the story of Abraham at the Oak of Mamre, when he received the 'honoured guests' in his tent – guests who were angels in guise. The biblical (Gen.18:1–8) and Qur'anic (Q51:24–30) versions are by and large

TIMELINE

1ST CENTURY CE	6TH CENTURY CE	10–11TH CENTURIES
Plutarch writes on table talk and food	Arab poet Hatem Ta`I known for his legendary hospitality and generosity	Al-Ghazali writes on food and hospitality in his *Ihya*

interpreted as positive stories of welcoming and offering space and shelter to the stranger or the traveller. Abraham's actions and his character are often used as an image of unity and common ground between Judaism, Christianity and Islam on the theme of hospitality. Some would claim that the fundamental moral practice of hospitality that welcomes the stranger is the essence of the three monotheistic religions.

The Qur'an and the Prophet's *sunna* often align hospitality with charity, in which the act of hospitality is framed largely in the act of giving. Giving was always seen as an act of hospitality and narratives often focused on the poor and poverty. Much of the Qur'anic emphasis is on giving to those in need, whether through tax, alms or charity, as a way of creating new relationships, and a new and more generous social order.

> **A HOUSE THAT IS NOT ENTERED BY GUESTS, IS NOT ENTERED BY ANGELS.**
> Al-Ghazali, d. 1111).

NOBILITY AND COMPASSION

The themes, and the people around which this ethical imperative to give and share is framed, are present in a pre-Islamic milieu. Bedouin societies laid an enormous emphasis on hospitality as being central to nobility of character. Generosity (*karam*) is part of hospitality and consists, first and foremost, in providing food. In its pre-modern and pre-industrial Arabian context, hospitality is regarded as something fundamental to the desert environment and nomadic wanderings.

It is also acknowledged that generosity and hospitality were themselves synonymous with the pre-Islamic concept of honour and that generosity and liberality towards guests and strangers were a mark of genuine nobility. We have several examples of individuals who reached the highest point of generosity and hospitality in the pre-Islamic period, the most famous and most proverbial being the Arab poet Hatim al-Ta'i. The only things that

1825

Jean Antheleme Brillat-Savarin's *The Physiology of Taste*

2014–16

Huge influx of migrants to Europe raises questions about hospitality

Eating lawfully

While Qur'anic proscriptions on what we eat are very few, eating lawful food is a theme that resonates in many genres of Islamic literature. This theme goes well beyond required ritual slaughter. What we eat carries meaning in this life and the next. Food is a universal human requirement for survival and not a sin of self-indulgence; rather, eating well and lawfully is encouraged as a blessing from God. This theme finds emphasis in the traditions pertaining to the Prophet's ascension narrative (mi`raj, see Chapter 19). Here, the Prophet witnesses a table spread with pieces of good meat that no one is eating and rotten meat that many are enjoying. When he asks the angel Jibril (Gabriel), who these people are, the reply is, 'These are of your community who abandon what is lawful and proceed to what is unlawful'.

Food becomes a potent metaphor for human actions and always reflects more than simply feeding ourselves. How and what we eat speaks of the connection between the physical, psychological and spiritual. In this context, Muhammad also witnesses a group of people whose lips resembled the lips of camels and who were being stoned. When he asks about these people, Jibril replies, 'They are those of your community who eat up the property of orphans and commit injustice. They are eating nothing but a fire in their bellies, and they shall be roasted in it'. Thus, punishments for the evils you commit in this life are reimagined as terrible forced consumption in the next.

Hatim did not give away through his generosity were his horse and his weapons. However, one bad year when the Earth was very dry and the crops had been wiped out and there was no food, Hatim killed his horse in response to his neighbour's cry for help to feed her children. His own children and others nearby also ate the meat, but he himself did not take a single bite.

In the writings of Muslim scholars, human generosity and magnanimity reflect God's nature, but in the actual practice of welcoming and receiving guests there are also limits to hospitality: limits and obligations on both the host and the guest. This is because hospitality is real, not an ideal. It is joyous, but also time-consuming. It can be both physically and emotionally demanding. Yet at the very basis of hospitality is a compassion that shakes our complacency and leads us to think about more generous ways of being with one another. Compassion creates empathy and has the power to reduce personal and social conflicts.

THE ROLE PLAYED BY FOOD

Perhaps the theme most associated with hospitality is that of food and eating. Life may be more than food and eating, but there is no life without food and eating. Thus the theological and philosophical significance of what we eat and who we eat with, connect the ordinary life with the higher life. There are overlapping discourses on food as a blessing to be shared with others and food as a means of enjoying the company of others. These are accompanied by multiple commandments to give charity and shelter, to feed others, to look after widows, neighbours, travellers and orphans. We must give and be generous because this is how God is and God's giving knows no limits. Hospitality is not about institutional charity, but rather a virtue or a combination of virtues that go beyond giving.

ONE'S ATTITUDE TO LIFE

Studies of hospitality from the perspective outlined above often target the questions of subject- and identity-formation through the welcoming of others and being welcomed. Hospitality is also explored in association with the cultural and the public, by being an issue of public space and how a self-identified sociality welcomes strangers, immigrants and refugees into one's country or territory. This concept is gaining momentum as globalization, increased migrancy and refugees emerging from multiple conflicts and wars have forced many to think about what it means to welcome someone as stranger or guest. But the overarching goal of hospitality as an act and as an attitude to life has always been radical transformation. Hospitality is not some quaint sentimentality; it is about who we become when we think about the ways in which God wants us to be with one another.

The condensed idea
Hospitality keeps the sacred alive in the ordinary

27 Halal and haram

The word *halal* technically refers to things and persons that are permitted to the believer. It is the antonym of *haram*, meaning 'that which is forbidden or prohibited'. In the Qur'an these words and their cognate terms are used to mean lawful and unlawful.

From the root *h-l-l*, the Qur'an uses the verb *ahalla* to indicate lawfulness where it is usually God who makes things lawful for the believers. It can also mean profane in the sense of 'not sacred'. Words derived from the root *h-r-m* not only refer to God making things unlawful (*harrama*), but also express ideas of impurity and sacredness especially when it comes to space. For example, the Kaaba is *al-bayt al-haram* (Q5:97; see Chapter 6), and Muslims undertaking the *hajj* pilgrimage enter sanctity by wearing the *ihram* (see Chapter 25). There are other meanings, implying prohibitions such as 'staying away from' or 'avoid', but *haram* is central to Muslim legal ethical debates about divine prohibition.

Later in the classical period, jurists derived a gradation of moral evaluation (*hukm/ahkam*) that went beyond the strict binary of *halal* and *haram*. All human acts had a place on this scale, which progressed from mandatory (*fard/wajib*), through recommended (*mandub*), merely permitted (*mubah*) and disapproved (*makruh*) to forbidden (*haram*). The first four are variations of that which is permitted (*halal*). While these terms became prevalent in scholarly legal speculation – replacing *halal* and *haram* as the two simple divisions – popular piety retained the principles of *halal/haram* as a way of giving Muslims a more simplified practical guidance to everyday living.

TIMELINE

1991	2009
Mainstream food manufacturers and industry actively pursue *halal*	KFC begin to sell *halal* chicken in many of its restaurants

WHAT IS LAWFUL?

Most Qur'anic declarations of lawfulness and unlawfulness refer to ritual laws, dietary laws and family laws. They are about relationships and a 'right' attitude to life, which, in turn is reflective of one's relationship with God. Thus, implicit in *halal* are concepts of ethical consumption, stewardship of the Earth and social justice. For example, God has made trade permissible but prohibited usury (Q2:275). Also:

> The food of those to whom the Book was given is lawful for you and your food for them. And so are the virtuous women of the believers and the virtuous women of those who received the scripture before you (Q5:5).

The special status accorded to the Jews and the Christians meant that their food was also made lawful, although there remains controversy over slaughtered meat. Rightful relationships with people and the Earth are intrinsic to a moral life. This is also conveyed in a long list of women with whom marriage is forbidden: 'Forbidden to you in marriage are your mothers, your daughters, yours sisters . . .' (Q4:23).

When it comes to food, there is encouragement, if not an obligation, for believers to eat rather than to create restrictions for themselves, 'O people, eat of what is on Earth lawful and good' (Q2:168). The necessity of bodily sustenance reminds the believers of their dependence on God and the emphasis in the Qur'an is on the awareness of food being part of God's bounties and blessings. God's desire is not to make things difficult for the believer and the Qur'an in its most literal reading prohibits only four things:

> He has only forbidden you carrion and blood and the flesh of swine and that which has been slaughtered to any other than God. But if one is

2011

Census logs
2.7 million Muslims
in the UK; UK *halal*
food industry worth
£2.6 billion

2016

Ninety per cent
of Muslims eat
halal meat

driven by necessity, neither craving nor transgressing, there is no sin, for God is most giving and most merciful (Q2:173).

Meat that has been slaughtered to a being other than God, dead meat, blood and pig appear to be the main scriptural prohibitions when it comes to dietary laws. Later on, wine and other intoxicating substances were also seen as prohibited.

> **EVERY CREATURE THAT LIVES SHALL BE YOURS TO EAT; I GIVE THEM ALL TO YOU AS I DID THE GREEN PLANTS. YOU MUST NOT HOWEVER, EAT FLESH WITH ITS LIFE BLOOD. FOR YOUR LIFE BLOOD TOO I WILL REQUIRE A RECKONING. WHOEVER SHEDS THE BLOOD OF MAN, FOR THAT MAN SHALL HIS BLOOD BE SHED. FOR IN THE IMAGE OF GOD WAS MAN CREATED.**
>
> Genesis 9:3–6, The Bible

ANIMAL WELFARE

Concerning meat, the task for the jurists was to explain the details of correct slaughter. This included close attention to what constituted ritually slaughtered meat and who was eligible to slaughter. Within these debates, classical law questioned whether the process of slaughter should be seen as an act of worship, especially as there was no unanimity as to whether pronouncing God's name over the animal was necessary. A close reading of these texts displays creative ingenuity rather than stringency in allowing people to eat meat even if not ritually slaughtered.

Muslim opinion, however, remains divided about stunning an animal both as an internal debate and in response to concerns expressed by animal rights organizations. There have been some formal pronouncements, including that of the rector of Al-Azhar University in Cairo, who stated in 1982 that if an animal becomes unconscious through stunning, it is technically still alive and slaughter can be carried out.

ETHICAL CONSUMERISM

Halal along with *kosher* is known as a religious term in most European societies and *halal* certification on food products has become common. Yet the values promoted by *halal*, such as social responsibility, stewardship of the Earth, economic and social justice and animal welfare, have gathered interest beyond religious compliance and the market has gained increasing acceptance among some non-Muslim consumers who associate *halal* with

The history of the pig

Most people know that Muslims and Jews don't eat pork. But the ban on eating pig has a longer, pre-Islamic history. The fifth-century historian Sozomenus wrote of Judaizing Arabs in the Arabian peninsula who refrained from the use of pork.

The taboo around pig meat has fascinated anthropologists and cultural ecologists for many years. For them, and indeed for us, the question is not that there is a scriptural prohibition on eating pig, but what is the history of the evolution of this prohibition across cultures. The pig taboo has no single explanation and its curious place in agricultural and cultural history has been observed by many over the centuries. Many theories have been put forward as to why the pig was banned and why it came to symbolize the ultimate unclean animal in Islam. These range from ecological, mythological and scientific concerns between clean and unclean meat to the simple defence by the faithful that this is a divine command.

Purity laws and dietary laws are kept largely distinct in Islam, although pig and blood blur the boundaries. Generally speaking, however, principle sources of defilement are more limited in Islam than in Jewish law. In Islam there is no temple cult or priesthood, and so many of the laws of purity and impurity are founded on the daily life of the common man. In Islam, purity laws in religious doctrine appear predominantly in laws relating to prayer or marriage.

ethical consumerism. Today, *halal* is a global industry estimated to be worth around USD2.3 trillion. The global *halal* market of 1.8 billion Muslims is no longer confined to food and food-related products, but has expanded to include pharmaceuticals, cosmetics, health products and medical devices.

In recent years, the market has also responded by offering *halal* travel, hospitality services and fashion. *Halal* may still retain a sense of the lawful, but it has also become a global opportunity.

The condensed idea
Purity and cleanliness are different concepts

28 Alcohol

The Qur'an contains several verses that warn believers of the harm in drinking alcohol, mentioned specifically as *khamr* (wine). There are many reasons given for the gradual prohibition on the consumption of intoxicants and most Muslim families and societies refrain from drinking alcohol completely. In certain Muslim countries, governments have rules on what is socially acceptable for those who do drink, including non-Mulsims.

During the pre-Islamic period, wine drinking was glorified both in society and by the pre-Islamic poets. The Qur'an mentions drinking wine on separate occasions:

They ask you concerning wine and gambling. Say in them is great sin and some profit for men; but the sin is greater than the profit. (Q2:219)

O you who believe! Wine and gambling [games of chance] and sacrificing to stones and [divination] by arrows are a disgrace, the works of Satan. So stay away from it so that you may flourish. Satan wants to cause enmity and hatred between you with wine and gambling and hinder you from the remembrance of God and prayer. Will you not then abstain? (Q5:90)

Such verses reflect that, while alcohol consumption was prevalent in the Near East, and its benefits recognized, it was condemned as doing more harm than good to the individual and to wider society.

TIMELINE

8000 BCE	5400 BCE	8TH CENTURY BCE
Earliest form of grape-based fermented drink found in Georgia with wine residue inside ceramic jar	Earliest chemically attested grape wine discovered in the northwestern Zagros Mountains, Asia	Literary references to wine in Homer

FORBIDDEN INTOXICANTS

The word most frequently used for wine is *khamr*, which comes from both the date palm and the grape vine. According to the Prophet, *khamr* also comes from honey, raisins and wheat and he forabade every intoxicant.

In the Qur'an, there are words other than *khamr* used to imply an intoxicating drink. One of the more common is *sakar*. Whereas *khamr* is used in both senses as wine to be shunned as well as wine that is a heavenly reward, it does not imply in itself a state of intoxication. *Sukr* however is used in the dominant sense of being in some state of inebriety, where the intellect has been distorted.

> ❝ ONE SHOULD ALWAYS BE DRUNK. THAT'S ALL THAT MATTERS . . . BUT WITH WHAT? WITH WINE, WITH POETRY, OR WITH VIRTUE, AS YOU CHOOSE. BUT GET DRUNK. ❞
> Charles Baudelaire, (1821–67)

A HINDRANCE TO PRAYER

For most Muslims, the most important reason for the gradual ban on alcohol was because one cannot approach prayer while intoxicated; remembrance of God requires sobriety, hence the Qur'anic verse:

> O you who have believed, do not approach prayer while you are intoxicated until you know what you are saying or in a state of *janaba*. (Q4:43)

Being intoxicated came to be seen as part of a longer list of natural bodily functions that defile, such as illness and sexual intercourse. The intoxicated believer, too, needs to be purified from his state of 'defilement' – that is, he needs to be sober again so that he can pray, fully aware of the words he is speaking. The Qur'an links together wine and gambling, then adds idols and divination arrows to the list to remind people to stay away from those things that interfere with God, prayer and maintaining a unified community of believers.

750 BCE	**12TH CENTURY CE**	**2001–2011**
Phoenician shipwrecks discovered with cargoes of wine still intact	Ibn Rushd collates various legal arguments as to why wine is forbidden	Sales of alcohol in the Middle East grow by 72 per cent

Selling alcohol

The classical jurists debated whether one could sell wine, because there is a saying from the Prophet that both drinking and selling wine are prohibited. In such sayings, wine is considered 'filth'. But others allowed its sale as long as one did not drink it.

Al-Tirmidhi wrote, 'God's messenger cursed ten people in connection with wine: the wine presser, the one who has it pressed, the one who drinks it, the one who conveys it, the one to whom it is conveyed, the one who serves it, the one who sells it, the one who benefits from the price paid for it, the one who buys it and the one for whom it is bought'. However, legal texts distinguish between consumption and sale.

Many Muslims who do not drink alcohol also see its sale as completely prohibited. In 2013, the British store Marks & Spencer, allowed its Muslim staff to refuse to serve customers buying alcohol or pork products. Muslim staff who did not wish to handle alcohol or pork were advised that they could request that customers choose another till at which to pay. This policy decision highlighted a split among the big food retailers over whether religious staff should be excused certain jobs. Some claimed that there was no reason why goods that were prohibited for consumption for religious or cultural reasons, could not be handled for sale to others.

Most legal schools developed the view that drinking wine was a crime and liable to punishment, that any amount of an intoxicating substance, small or large, is prohibited. Others argued that it is being in a state of intoxication that is prohibited.

HEAVENLY DELIGHTS

The Qur'an also contains names of drinks that are part of a sensual image referring to divine mercy or divine reward. Images of rivers of milk and honey and pure, non-intoxicating wines in the form of *tasnim* and *rahiq*, dominate the popular imagination of heavenly delights. In the Qur'anic heaven, there will be various distinct flows of drinks and 'wines' in which *tasnim* appears to enjoy the most elevated status. All of these different drinks are united by being pure, which essentially means non-intoxicating, as opposed to the effect with ordinary wines.

The Qur'an presents no definitive understanding of the various drinks that are only partially encapsulated in the English translation of 'wine', but heavenly wine is the reward for abstention from earthly wine.

A CRIME AGAINST GOD

The Qur'anic discourse on any drink that has the potential to intoxicate is poised between the appreciation of those very drinks that were part of Arab cultural and social life, and a clear warning that intoxication leads to both forgetfulness of God and corruption of prayers as well as social discord. For the believing community, it was indeed the remembrance of God and obedience to his commands that defined and united them.

When one explores the various arguments around wine and alcohol in Islamic thought, it appears that what were considered 'benefits' of wine, were gradually eclipsed by repeating the problems that lay with consumption of wine. Layer upon layer of interpretation combined to magnify both drinking and the status of intoxication as subversive, ritually impure and, most importantly, a crime against God. While there is no punishment for drinking alcohol in any form in the Qur'an it was seen as a crime against God (*hadd*) in the legal manuals and liable to punishment by flogging.

Despite some divergence of views in Islamic law, abstention from alcohol has been regarded as a marker of piety and obedience throughout Islamic history. Some Muslims are wary of consuming alcohol in medicine or using cosmetics that contain alcohol. For others, it can also be a barrier to social bonding in Western cultures, where drinking is central to recreation and entertainment.

The condensed idea
Wine remains a legal problem for Muslims

29 The Prophet's wives

From the Qur'an and the Prophet's biographical literature, we learn about the Prophet's wives. He is said to have had 14 wives beginning with Khadijah and ending with Umm Salama. They are known as the 'mothers of the believers', and all but two of his marriages took place after his migration to Medina.

The Prophet's wives are esteemed figures in the Qur'an and in Muslim piety. The Qur'an addresses itself to the Prophet's wives on several occasions, linking their dignity and special status with heightened moral responsibility. However, the work never identifies any of them by name. The *hadith* literature and Qur'anic exegesis fills this gap, but Muhammad's wives are not mentioned equally. It is difficult to generalize about the marriages, as some of these unions strengthened political and tribal loyalties while other marriages were based on love and attraction.

A WIFE'S ROLE

Muhammad's first marriage was at the age of 25 to the 40-year-old Khadijah. She was a wealthy businesswoman who had hired him to trade for her, but who was drawn to his sincerity and success and eventually offered herself in marriage to him. He remained in a happy and monogamous marriage to Khadijah until her death, after which he is believed to have had multiple wives. With the exception of Aisha, his youngest wife who was only nine at the time the marriage was consummated, Muhammad only married widows and divorced women or captives. According to medieval commentators, Aisha was the Prophet's favourite wife and married him

TIMELINE

620 CE	622 CE
Muhammad's first wife Khadijah dies	Muhammad marries Aisha

three years before his migration to Medina. Aisha is reputed to have been very scholarly, a transmitter of thousands of *hadiths* and an authority in various fields of learning, such as medicine. She was one of two wives given an apartment adjoining the Prophet's mosque in Medina.

Muslim commentators state that Muhammad's wives participated fully in society until the *hijab* verse (see page 124), which ascribed a level of seclusion from public life. Thus, the Prophet's wives were given privilege and an elite status. They contributed in different ways, his later wives accompanying him in wars and battles – not as fighters, but as women who offered physical and emotional support to the Prophet's cause. Muhammad's widow Hafsa bint Umar played a role in the collection of the first Qur'anic manuscript. It is said that after Abu Bakr had collected the copy, he gave it to Hafsa, who preserved it until Uthman took this version and, after making multiple copies, distributed them across Muslim lands.

> **AND OF HIS SIGNS IS THAT HE CREATED FOR YOU MATES FROM AMONG YOURSELVES, SO THAT YOU MAY FIND TRANQUILLITY IN THEM; AND HE PLACED BETWEEN YOU AFFECTION AND MERCY.**
> Q30:21

MUHAMMAD'S HOUSEHOLD

While classical works speak, to some extent, of Muhammad's sexual relationship with his wives and his commitment to treating them all as fairly as possible, these works also portray a varied picture of the Prophet's household. It is one in which ordinary human jealousies and rivalries are naturally present, although such images have faded in popular piety today.

Muhammad's wives are exalted as being archetypes of feminine virtue, support and righteousness. The emphasis on family life and the domestic skills become exemplary attributes of womanhood. Furthermore, according to the Qur'an, God forbade anyone to marry the wives of Muhammad following his death, out of respect and honour for them.

625 CE

Muhammad marries Hafsa bin Umar, who is widowed at the Battle of Badr

680 CE

Umm Salama, Muhammad's last wife, lives through the tragedy of Karbala and dies the same year

Polygamy in Britain

Recent studies of the lives of Muslim women in the UK conclude that many women are trapped in polygamous marriages, while others are choosing to enter a polygamous relationship. Those in the former category are not always aware of their husband's marital situation because, often, the other wives live in separate accommodation.

Muslim couples often marry through the *nikah* ceremony only, and are unaware that they need to register their marriage at a civil court for it to have legal recognition in Britain. While polygamy is practised by less than five per cent of Muslims worldwide, there are some women in the UK who are choosing to enter a polygamous relationship as a lifestyle choice. There are women who wish to pursue a career, yet still have a male partner in their lives; for them a polygamous relationship works well, even though it is not recognized as being legally valid under UK law. While Muslim women's organizations often speak out against polygamous marriages, it is frequently justified by some who believe that men are polygamous by nature.

However co-wives are often in vulnerable positions. If a marriage breaks down, they have no legal or financial protection, because this kind of marriage is not recognized under UK law. Sharia law has no jurisdiction in the United Kingdom so attempting to enter legally into a polygamous marriage in the UK is a criminal offence that can carry a maximum sentence of seven years in prison.

THE CONCEPT OF POLYGAMY

That Muhammad's household was polygamous has historically led to two particular ways of thinking about polygamy. The first is to defend it on the basis that, as an institution rightly practised, it can offer compassion and protection to women who are left vulnerable for a variety of reasons:

> And if you fear that you may not be just to the orphans, then you may marry whom you please of the women: two, and three, and four. But if you fear you will not be fair, then only one, or what your right hand possesses. This is best that you do not face financial hardship. (Q 4:3)

While this verse raises several questions about slave ownership, as well as marriage to free women, it became the main focus for discussions around the legal validity of polygamy in Muslim societies. For many reformers, however, polygamy had once been a useful historical necessity, but had been corrupted and had no place in modernity. The Egyptian writer Muhammad Abduh (d. 1905) called for the abolition of polygamy, arguing that it was little more than a licence for male lust and female oppression. Its original aim of providing equity and justice had disappeared and it no longer contributed to the welfare of Muslim societies.

THE CHRISTIAN VIEW

Muhammad's multiple marriages became a central motif in medieval Christian polemics against Islam. Whereas Muslims claimed that Muhammad's call was life-affirming both physically and spiritually, to some Christians, he represented the opposite of true spirituality.

Thomas Aquinas (1225–74) was an Italian Dominican priest of the Roman Catholic Church and one of the West's most influential philosophers and theologians. When addressing Islam, he was keen to stress that the 'truths' Muhammad brought were fundamentally doctrines mixed with falsehoods with no divine supernatural quality. Such teachings appealed to desert wanderers but also those for whom carnal pleasures were an attraction. Muhammad's sexual prowess contrasted with Jesus's sexual abstinence. Islam, unlike Christianity, promised people sexual and other pleasures as a reward for virtue, whereas Christianity offered eternal bliss. Such polemics continue to be part of those levelled against Muhammad, even today, in the broader Islam/West debates.

The condensed idea
Polygamy within Muslim societies is hotly debated

30 Mary

In both Christianity and Islam, Mary or Maryam is the mother of Jesus. In Islam, Mary's story is an example of virtue, obedience and purity 'an example of the righteous'. (Q66:12) She is a figure with a lasting appeal in both religions. Many see her as an inspiring and reconciling figure between the past and the present and between the feminine and the feminine ideal.

The Qur'an only has one *sura* named after a woman – *sura* 19 or *sura Maryam*. It is a chapter dedicated to Mary, the mother of Jesus, the most chaste and virtuous woman, and the one who receives an angelic annunciation of a pure son from God's spirit – a word from God cast unto Mary. In the Qur'an, only Moses, Abraham and Noah are mentioned by name more frequently than Mary, and Mary herself is mentioned more times in the Qur'an than in the Bible's entire New Testament. There are 70 verses that refer to her and she is mentioned specifically in 34 of these. She is an example for the believers:

> God has chosen you and purified you and chosen you above women of all peoples. (Q3:42)

WHO WAS MARY?

Mary's story is mysterious and is found within the few references to her in the Qur'an. Her mother is not mentioned by name in the Qur'an but referred to as the 'wife of Imran'. Islamic tradition has given her

TIMELINE

610–622 CE	9TH CENTURY CE
Nineteenth chapter of Qur'an names *sura Maryam*	Bartholomew of Edessa writes about reverence for Mary in the Qur'an

the name Hanna and she is considered to be a sister to Elizabeth (Zakariah's wife and the mother of John the Baptist). Before Mary's birth, her mother pledges to consecrate her unborn child to God's service.

This is a curious pledge, as women were not considered appropriate for servanthood in a house of worship. This was partly because of menstrual impurity and the limitations on men and women mixing in a place of worship. When Mary is born, she serves in the sanctuary of the temple, which emphasizes a separate physical location in which she could devote herself to worship, a place where men had no access. Mary stays there under the care of Zakariah, who is always surprised to find her receiving food miraculously and when he asks her how, she replies, 'It is from God. Indeed, God provides for whom he wills without account'. (Q3:37)

> CONSIDERED IN HIS MORTAL FORM, ONE MIGHT SAY THAT HE IS THE SON OF MARY. CONSIDERED IN HIS FORM OF HUMANITY, ONE MIGHT SAY THAT HE IS OF GABRIEL, WHILE CONSIDERED WITH RESPECT TO THE REVIVAL OF THE DEAD, ONE MIGHT SAY THAT HE IS OF GOD AS SPIRIT.
>
> Ibn al-`Arabi (1165–1240)

A WOMAN OF TRUTH

There are two annunciation stories in the Qur'an. One of them has the 'spirit of God', assumed to be Jibril (Gabriel), sent to her 'in the form of a perfected man' to tell her news of the gift of a 'pure son'. Mary's fear is that she has been chaste all her life but now will be shamed in front of her people. She is reassured that her son, Jesus, is a mercy from God. When she gives birth and people see her, they accuse her of unchastity but Jesus replies that he is a prophet of God and that 'Peace was on me the day I was born and will be on me the day I die and the day I am raised to life again'. (Q19: 16-34) Mary's pregnancy and Jesus's birth are God's will and the Qur'an proclaims several times that Mary is among the 'devoutly obedient' of God's servants and a 'woman of truth'. (Q5:75)

1968
Vision of Mary reported in Cairo's *al-Ahram* newspaper.

1988
Mosque Maryam built in Chicago, Illinois, by Nation of Islam

A Persian depiction of Mary, Jesus and the Palm Tree, a story featured in the Qur'an but not in the canonical Bible.

In Islam, Marian piety is not Advent piety. The Islamic tradition regards Mary's position as unique, but her piety has a limited role and no continuing role in eschatology. Sufi poets, such as Rumi, drew on the figures of Mary and Jesus, comparing man's spirit to Jesus and his body to Mary – that one must endure the pains of the body to develop the spirit of Jesus. But such writings always drew a distinction between the Christian and Muslim views of Mary and Jesus. Mary's work was complete with Christ's birth and the mission of doing God's new work lies with Christ and not Mary.

MARY, THE VIRGIN

While the Qur'an emphasizes Mary's chastity and purity, with Islam affirming Mary's immaculate conception and the virginal birth, Muslim theology has not regarded sexual purity as a desired aspect of righteous femininity. Chastity before marital relations became morally and legally significant, but it did not equate to an obsession for sexual purity as being a divine ideal – lawful sex is never sinful. Furthermore, Mary's pure and virginal motherhood have not made the status of ordinary motherhood any less important. It could be argued that motherhood has remained the most virtuous and socially desirable role for Muslim women.

The doctrinal density associated with Mary in Christian thought has no equivalence in Islam. Mary is given a special status in the Qur'an but in the Islamic tradition, it is Fatima, the Prophet's daughter – and the mother of the tragic heroes, Hassan and Hussain, the Prophet's grandsons – who in popular piety is venerated above Mary.

A COMFORT TO WOMEN

Today, *sura Maryam* continues to be read by women across the Muslim world when they are pregnant or praying for some solace in their lives; it is a *sura* that confers special blessings and has retained a significance across communities in the Muslim world.

Mary as reconciling figure

Mary is revered by many in popular Islamic piety, but she is not the mother of God. In Islam, she does not have the same role that she has for Roman Catholic Christianity or indeed the Theotokos, 'the one who gave birth to the one who is God', according to one of her titles in Eastern Christianity. Confirmed by the Church at the Council of Ephesus in 431, but going back as far as the time of Origen (d. 254), this has long been her title.

Mary lives in daily piety within Muslim and Christian communities. Indeed, one could argue that her presence haunts those who desire to see her. 'She appeared on several nights, in different forms – sometimes in full body, at other times only half – surrounded by a halo of bright light. Sometimes she would appear in the domes of the church above'. This was the description of the appearance of the Virgin Mary, published in Cairo's *Al-Ahram* paper in May 1968. Muslims and Christians flocked to see this vision.

In 1988, Cardinal Arinze of the Vatican's secretariat for non-Christians addressed a greeting to Muslims, whom he called brothers and sisters in God. He quoted Mary, 'the mother of Jesus whom both Christians and Muslims – without according her the same role and title – honour as a model for believers'. Even the earliest Christian respondents to Islam such as Bartholomew of Edessa (*c.* 13th century) wrote that Mary was praised more in the Qur'an than the Prophet or his mother Aminah.

The condensed idea
Mary might have been considered a prophet

31 Hijab, niqab and burqa

Women wearing the *hijab* (headcovering) or the *niqab* (full-face veil) have become one of the most visible signs of Islam in Europe and the West. While those who wear the *hijab/niqab*, defend these coverings as a command of God, many others state that this is not a religious obligation, but rather a cultural legacy of seventh-century Arabia.

The Qur'an contains various verses in which the word *hijab*, literally a screen or curtain, is used to convey a sense of separation. The concept of separation conveyed in *hijab* is used in a variety of ways and instances, including an example in which Mary withdraws from her family and placing a screen (to screen herself) from the others (Q19:17). Separation is most strikingly used to describe the manner in which God sends revelation, which he sends through inspiration, prophets and from 'behind a veil' (Q42:51). This concept of a hidden, unknowable, yet revealing God remains a powerful image in Islamic theological and Sufi literature.

MODESTY VERSES

The verse most famously known as the *hijab* verse refers more specifically to the observance of certain manners when in the company of the Prophet:

> O believers, do not enter the Prophet's house unless permission is given to you for a meal, and if you ask them [the Prophet's wives] for something you need, ask them from behind a *hijab*, that is purer for your hearts. (Q33:53)

TIMELINE

1922	2006
Pioneering Egyptian feminist, Huda Sha'arawi, removes her veil in public	Jack Straw, UK politician, calls the *niqab* 'a statement of separation'

The verses around this commandment prescribe a level of seclusion for the Prophet's wives, away from public gaze. The famous 'mantle verse' addresses itself to the Prophet, saying that he should tell his wives and daughters and the believing women to cover themselves in a cloak when outside, so that they are recognized in the streets by their clothing and not molested.

These verses are linked to the 'modesty' verses, which tell the believing men 'to lower their gaze and guard their private parts' (Q24:30). Muslim women are also advised to do the same and also not to 'display their adornments except for what is apparent, and let them draw their covering over their bosoms and not to display their adornments except to their husbands, their fathers' (Q24:31).

> **THE BEST PROTECTION AGAINST RAPE, STALKING AND DOMESTIC VIOLENCE IS TO RAISE MEN WHO BOTH UNDERSTAND THAT WOMEN ARE DIFFERENT, AND WOULD NEVER DARE TAKE ADVANTAGE OF THIS DIFFERENCE.**
> Wendy Shalit (b. 1975)

Such verses gave rise to a diversity of opinion about modesty, covering and seclusion. While some claim that the Prophet's wives were privileged women for whom greater seclusion from the public was necessary, others claim that whatever was prescribed for the Prophet's wives, should be binding on all Muslim women. Suffice it to say that, despite some agreements among scholars, that women should be covered, as part of the wider debates on sexual modesty, there was no agreed dress code.

FAITH AND IDENTITY

The word *hijab* has evolved in meaning and over the last century, and is now most commonly used to denote the idea of a Muslim woman's covering. It has come to symbolize faith and identity in a powerful and politicized way. Women's clothing was traditionally about women's honour, but is now seen by some as reflecting women's choices and empowerment. Empowerment and freedom gave rise to multiple ways of thinking about veiling. In the 19th century, Arabs who had either visited or been educated in the West, such as

2010

French ban on face covering (*niqab*) in public

2013

Nazma Khan founds World *Hijab* Day, February 1st

Veiling and unveiling

Many observers state that the full-face veil, the *niqab*, is a way of excluding women from the public sphere. When a woman's face is invisible, she is invisible. But clothing has been a contested issue in understanding male patriarchy and female autonomy for centuries.

A woman's body has always been subject to control or regulation by men. In a work entitled *Scheherazade Goes West*, the Moroccan anthropologist, Fatema Mernissi, makes a witty comment in taking up the debate of how attitudes to clothing reflect both the Western man and the Muslim man's appreciation or degradation of a woman's beauty. Mernissi's argument is that it is patriarchal control that determines how beauty is imagined and preserved. In a conversation with her friend Jacques, who is showing her the museums and art galleries of Paris and who insists that the women in his harem must be 'nude and silent' she replies:

Muslim men seem to get a virile power from veiling women and harassing them in the streets if they aren't 'covered' properly, while Western men like yourself seem to derive a tremendous pleasure from unveiling them.

Qasim Amin and Rifa'a al-Tahtawi, targeted particular issues. In their own way, they championed what they saw as opening new avenues for women. Amin focused on the veil and female seclusion in general as indicative of the social backwardness of Islamic societies. Unless women were educated in a formal sense, Arab society would not truly prosper. Huda Sha`arawi (d. 1947), the founder of the Egyptian Feminist Union, was to emphasize this unease with the veil even more when she took the veil off in public on her return from the International Union of Women in Rome.

WESTERN VIEWS

Veiling in all its forms, whether it is the *hijab*, the *niqab* or the full outer garment (the *burqa*) has become a central feature when discussing Islam in the West. Gender segregation – whether portable or physical – is seen by many Muslims as the expression of an ideal Muslim life. It has also rather curiously become part of the human rights discourse in the UK, under the section of the European Convention relating to religious belief. The argument by many is that the *niqab* symbolizes a barrier to open communication and the equal place of women in public life. Rather than convincing the onlooker that it is about a woman's right to practise her faith as she understands it, this covering has become a symbol of denying women their full humanity. Whether one agrees with those perspectives that argue for or against female veiling within religiosity or human rights, the debate has become one of the most politically charged expressions of religious otherness today.

INCREASING VISIBILITY

The increasing visibility of the *hijab* and the *niqab* has become an embattled area in the field of Islam and feminism, with both academic discourse and popular voices presenting a spectrum of views challenging Eurocentric liberalism and advocating an indigenous feminism. But the veil in all its forms is worn for a variety of reasons in both Muslim and non-Muslim countries. Its increasing visibility has created a whole new fashion industry and become part of a social and religious reality for many women.

The condensed idea
Modesty is part of Islam

32 Women and equality

The discussions around women in Islam and in Muslim society remain some of the most contested and generalized in both popular and academic debates. A common understanding is that while the Qur'an largely gives spiritual egalitarianism to both men and women, it remains a sacred text that, like other scriptures including the Bible, has historically been used legally and socially to favour men.

Gender relations lie at the very heart of society and how society behaves spiritually, psychologically, socially and economically. Conversations about women and gender-related issues in Islam have been dominated by concerns of rights and justice. As the world has moved gradually towards the discourse of individual rights and social justice, this is hardly surprising.

WOMEN IN THE QUR'AN

Diverse feminist perspectives highlight the reality of women's lives in many parts of the Islamic world. These either critique patriarchal structures or explain Qur'anic verses according to their seventh-century contexts. Almost without exception, they maintain that, contrary to popular perception, there are no identified roles for women in the Qur'an. They argue that the Qur'an gives spiritual egalitarianism to both men and women, however unequal or unjust social structures might be.

Righteousness knows no gender boundaries in the Qur'an. As it says, 'As for those who lead a righteous life, male or female, while believing, they

TIMELINE

12TH CENTURY	1923	1949
Ibn al-Arabi writes of the Ideal Man as both male and female	Huda Sha`arawi, founder and first president of Egyptian Feminist Union removes face veil in public	Simone de Beauvoir's *The Second Sex*

enter Paradise; without the slightest injustice' (Q4:124). The various themes in the Qur'an appear far less concerned with defining men and women in terms of the socially constructed gender traits of masculinity and femininity or binary expressions of sexual differences. In fact, the Qur'an seldom speaks of women as a collective. It is a text far more concerned with the moral dimensions of people's relationships to each other and their relationship with God.

A FEMINIST VIEW

Notwithstanding the struggle for rights in many parts of the Islamic world, contemporary feminist exegetes are concerned with advocating a more holistic treatment of the Qur'an and a dynamic open-endedness of interpretation. They have tended to prioritize general principles over particular statements – for example, the much-used verse 'Men are the maintainers of women' (Q4:34), which has been the subject of intense legal and hermeneutical debates for decades. Some

Divorce

Divorce in Islamic law is usually called *talaq*. But this word in itself does not always mean an immediate dissolution of the contract, only an intention to dissolve the marriage contract. The English word 'divorce' can be misleading, therefore, when translating the Arabic *talaq*. This is because 'divorce' denotes a termination of matrimonial relations between husband and wife, while the *talaq* is regarded fundamentally as a process of repudiation, possibly leading to a final dissolution of the marriage contract.

The exception to this in Hanafi law may be when divorce is pronounced before the husband has consummated the marriage with his wife. Yet, while divorce is regarded as the thing most hated by God and to be avoided if at all possible, the innovative divorce or the triple divorce – that is, where a man can say 'I divorce you' three times in a row – was considered unlawful at first by most of the Sunni schools but came to be accepted as sinful though legally valid. Despite clear Qur'anic injunctions to the contrary, immediate triple divorce is permitted, destroying marital life almost instantly. The practice of immediate triple divorce is widespread among Sunni Muslims, and despite being controversial, has legal validity. The dispute has been highlighted by reports of some Muslims instantly divorcing their wives by mail, over the telephone and even through text messages. Many women's organizations argue that this kind of unethical freedom of men gradually chisels away at the rights women have struggled for over the centuries.

1956
Tunisian law bans polygamy

1999
Amina Wadud's *Qur'an and Woman*

> **I RAISE UP MY VOICE – NOT SO I CAN SHOUT, BUT SO THAT THOSE WITHOUT A VOICE CAN BE HEARD . . . WE CANNOT SUCCEED WHEN HALF OF US ARE HELD BACK.**
>
> Malala Yousafzai (b. 1997)

Muslim feminist writers assert that the Qur'an gave rights and recognition to women as women, and not as unequal beings in any way. Yet, many argue that these rights have been easily ignored or subsumed in patriarchal legal codes or cultures in which male authority remains largely unquestioned.

Asma Barlas repudiates the patriarchal view of God and argues that even though the seventh-century context of a patriarchal Arabia was the context of the Qur'an, this was a historical contingency and does not mean that the same norms have to be upheld. Yet others, like Raja Rhouni, critique the project of retrieval, of uncovering gender equality as a norm by Muslim feminists. The concern for them is that as long as the Qur'an is seen as the repository of truths, from which an egalitarian Islam can always be retrieved, feminist exegesis will continue to explain away difficult verses on the basis of historical contingency, while accepting others of a more progressive nature.

CHALLENGING DISCRIMINATION

The emphasis on the struggle for recognition, justice and respect for women – as well as that most elusive ideal, equality – is a modern discourse. The classical traditions of most religions, including Islam, while trying to give and protect certain rights for women, were not unduly concerned with rights and equality in the ways that prevail today.

Our awareness of equality and justice issues has changed hugely in the last few decades, primarily owing to a focus on individual rights. Yet, while many struggles remain everywhere in the world, there are some milestones. For example, in the second half of the 20th century, through the UN Convention on the Elimination of all forms of Discrimination against Women (CEDAW), gender equality acquired a clearer and more urgent international mandate. This kind of international agreement, however contested and effective, still speaks of an aspiration towards a different kind of ethics, in which a moral imperative for justice for all demands listening to all.

MODERN-DAY WOMEN AND ISLAM

Despite the reality of issues that include forced marriages, polygamy and honour killings, to which women remain the most vulnerable, there is great diversity in the voices and experiences of Muslim women in the modern world. Women often negotiate their faith and their rights in more sophisticated and nuanced ways in Islamic societies. One area in which women seem to have exercised relative autonomy is in medieval Sufism. Many Sufi women – like their male contemporaries – lived independently, travelled on their own in search of knowledge and had both male and female teachers and disciples. It is also worth mentioning that, in the area of transmitting knowledge or acquiring expertise in the religious sciences, such as *hadith* scholarship, many women achieved relatively high status in early and medieval Islam. Their names are mentioned in biographical collections and it is recognized that part of their learning required contact with men. Yet, it is also true that their learning hardly ever translated into teaching in formal positions in Islamic institutions.

Aside from the scriptures, archival research into the lives of ordinary Muslim women frequently reveals a varied balance of power and public visibility. There is often a disconnect between legal texts, which imagine women as victims rather than active participants who are socially and legally aware, able to make their own decisions and challenge the prevailing injustice. The heterogeneity of the Muslim world – that is, the different voices, moralities and lifestyles – are completely lost in many of the generalizations made about women and Islam. Simply put, there is no one way to be a Muslim woman.

The condensed idea
Male–female equality
remains a revolutionary idea

33 Sex and sexuality

Islamic thought recognizes and celebrates human sexuality in both men and women and gives them rights over each other while creating a legal framework for lawful sex. To be human is to desire, and human sexuality is seen as one of our greatest driving impulses.

Islam views human sexuality, desire and erotic love as intrinsic to the fullness of human experience. The Qur'anic verses acknowledge and celebrate the presence of sexuality in all of humankind because we are created as sexual beings and very quickly understand the power of the sexual impulse. The famous theologian jurist al-Ghazali (d. 1111) argued that God had created us as sexual beings and that sexual desire was an inescapable feature of human minds and bodies. Yet, it is precisely because the sexual impulse is so powerful that sexual relations are commended within licit frameworks.

MARRIAGE IN ISLAM

Marriage remains the only legal sexual relationship outside of the classical rules on concubinage within the rules of slavery. While Islamic cultures vigorously extol the virtue and importance of marriage, there is no command to marry in the Qur'an itself, even if there is a strong directive in both the Qur'an and the *hadith* literature that marriage is a desirable and practicable state for a good Islamic life. While the Qur'an addresses the question as to those with whom marriage is and is not permitted, the closest we get to an actual encouragement to marry is contained in the

TIMELINE

7TH CENTURY CE	10–11TH CENTURIES
Qu'ranic verses acknowledge sexuality in all mankind	Al-Ghazali argues that God created humankind as sexual beings

verse, 'You shall encourage those of you who are single to get married' (Q24:32). Indeed, the marriage contract (*nikah*) means sexual intercourse.

The virtues and pleasures of marriage are discussed in the wider theological literature, in which sexual need – particularly male sexual desire – is considered a dominant reason for marrying, as this desire is too powerful an impulse and too great a distraction from service to God.

No defined role

The Qur'an remains silent on the woman as homemaker and does not define any domestic roles for women within the marriage. This is a relationship that assumes the freedoms of both partners and their abilities to act autonomously. There is no comparison made between male and female as sexual beings or as sexual partners in their private or public lives. Yet, this did not stop the Islamic tradition from carving out particular ways of thinking about how Muslim women should behave.

Although much of the jurisprudential debate on marriage in Islam looked at the sexual and contractual nature of this union, Islamic discussions of marriage in the classical and modern period have generally focused on faithful marriage as essential to family life and societal good. The complexity of human desire has focused largely on heterosexual marriage as providing the divinely sanctioned context for a sexual life. In marriage, two people can share the mutuality of physical and emotional needs and thus marriage without consummation – that is, without the mutual enjoyment of sex – has no real place in Islamic law and society. Sexual transgression, for example, adultery, breaks the bonds of fidelity and licit sex, and is seen as going against God's desired moral order.

The affirmation of sexuality and the sexual impulse is implicit in the marriage contract, but so is recognition that the sexual exists within the ethics of modesty. Modesty and sexuality contain a certain, even

1858

The Ottoman Caliph decriminalizes homosexuality in Turkey

2013

Shereen El Feki publishes *Sex and the Citadel: Intimate Life in a Changing Arab World*

WHERE THERE IS LIFE, THERE IS DESIRE.
Abdelwahab Bouhdiba

paradoxical, sacredness in the Islamic tradition, as both are regarded as fundamental to the ideal of an Islamic society. In several verses, the Qur'an has a particular taxonomy of actions that places fasting, remembrance of God and 'guarding of private parts' in the same category.

These categories of rightful behaviour are incumbent on men and women. This reflects a particular ethic in which the boundaries between the earthly and the transcendental come together in the virtue ethics of the Qur'an. Thus, performing rituals, such as fasting, remembering God and retaining chaste behaviour, are all aspects of worship. In a religion in which clothing has, for many, retained a central place in defining the ideal image of Muslim piety and modesty, the Qur'anic verses that speak of husband and wife as 'being garments for one another' are a potent and demanding depiction of complementarity. Marriage is a guardian of modesty for both.

SEXUAL ABSTINENCE

Throughout Islamic history, there has been considerable focus on chastity and sexual abstinence before marriage as a pious ideal. But Islamic history and contemporary Islamic societies show that it remains just that – an ideal. While virginity and abstinence before marriage are commended as fundamental to a moral life, there is a complex history of sex and sexuality in Islamic societies.

The Arab writer Joseph Massad has surveyed a wide range of literature, including the psychoanalytical, to show how one group of people – the Arabs – represented their own sexual desires. The variety of sexual behaviour in practice in Arab societies and in literature, challenges Western binary perceptions that Islamic societies have been either very prude or very licentious. Those scholars re-evaluating the more complex histories of Muslim societies, argue that there was once an openness in Islamic societies that gradually became corrupted by the practice of the segregation of the sexes, which in turn led to the rise of promiscuity.

HOMOSEXUALITY IN ISLAM

Homosexual relations remain a contested area of sexual ethics, and many Muslim countries condemn homosexuality as a crime. Such views are based most commonly on Qur'anic reference to the 'lewd' transgression of Lot's people (Q7:80–81).

Homosexual activity can receive state punishment, including the death penalty in some countries. Even though heterosexual and homosexual relationships both exist within society, very often gay Muslims are forced to live double lives. In recent years, many voices have emerged from within the Islamic world calling for a more sympathetic reading of those verses that have traditionally been used to condemn homosexual relations. The arguments posed by many who write on sex and sexuality is that, in early Islam, there was an openness about issues to do with sexuality that subsequently gave way to a more repressed debate on sexuality.

Powerful literary women

The famous tales of *A Thousand and One Nights* centre on the intelligent and beautiful Scheherazade. Scheherazade's tale is the ultimate tale of a woman overpowering her master, not with her beauty or wiles, but with her intellect and charm. The grief-stricken king Shahryar kills his wife after he discovers her infidelity. In revenge he wants to sleep with a virgin every night and then kill her. But his vizier's daughter, Scherazade begins to tell the king a tale, but does not end it. The king, curious about how the story ends, is thus forced to postpone her execution in order to hear the conclusion. The next night, as soon as she finishes the tale, she begins (and only begins) a new one, and eager to hear the conclusion, the king postpones her execution once again. So it goes on for 1,001 nights. By the end, he has fallen in love with her.

The condensed idea
Lawful sex is not sinful

34 The Qur'an

The Qur'an is central to the Muslim faith, serving as both scripture and guidance. The word *qur'an* literally means 'recitations' or 'the reciting'. Muslims regard the Qur'an as the very word of God revealed to his last Prophet, Muhammad (*c.* 570–632 CE), through the medium of the angel Jibril (Gabriel).

It is said that, in 610 CE, when Muhammad was around 40 years of age, he began to withdraw to the outskirts of Mecca to mediate. During one of his mediations, in the cave of Hira, the angel Jibril came to him and asked him to read. The following is one of the traditional accounts of how the first revelation took place:

> The angel came to him and asked him to read. The Prophet replied, 'I do not know how to read'. The Prophet added, 'The angel caught me and pressed me so hard that I could not bear it any more. He then released me and again asked me to read and I replied, "I don't know how to read". Thereupon he caught me again and pressed me a second time, until I could not bear it any more. He then released me and again asked me to read, but again I replied, "I do not know how to read". Thereupon, he caught me for the third time and pressed me, and then released me and said, "Read in the name of your Lord, who created man from a clot"'.

This is considered to be the first word of God or revelation brought to Muhammad by Jibril.

TIMELINE

610 CE	632 CE
Muhammad receives first revelation	Death of Muhammad

A HEAVENLY BOOK

A complete Qur'an is believed to be preserved on a heavenly tablet (*lawh al-mahfouz*) in the realm of eternity. Scholars of the Qur'an claim that the Qur'an as we know it took place in three stages. First, from God to the 'Preserved Tablet', a tablet that is also referred to as the Mother of the Book (*Umm al-Kitab*). For Muslims, this refers to an original heavenly book, and the archetype in which all earthly revelations – including the Qur'an as well as the Jewish and Christian scriptures – have their origin. Secondly, the Qur'an was sent from the highest heaven to the lowest heaven; thirdly, it was sent or 'revealed' via Jibril to Muhammad gradually over a period of around 22 years.

SPREADING THE WORD

Revelation was transmitted orally to Muhammad's followers, who memorized his words by heart or wrote them on palm branches, stones, animal skin or papyrus. Thus, on Muhammad's death in 632 CE, copies of various sections of the Qur'an were in existence, but there was no 'copy' of the Qur'an as a compiled book. The process of compiling a written version of

Interpreting the Qur'an

It is common to hear the Qur'an being recited in public places in Muslim societies. Muslims learn to read Qur'anic Arabic in order to read the Qur'an in its original language. Many Muslims learn proper elocution of Qur'anic Arabic, called *tajwid*. However, the Qur'an is also understood in translation by millions of Muslims.

One of the most common mistakes made by non-Muslims, is to confuse text and interpretation. The Qur'anic Arabic text has remained largely unchanged throughout history, while the Qur'an has been open to varying interpretations by scholars from the very beginning. Revelation always requires human reception, context and understanding. So while Muslims claim that the Qur'an is inimitable and preserved by God, interpretation has been an ongoing historical and theological process.

The exegesis of the Qur'an is called *tafsir*, and some of the most famous scholars in Islamic history were also exegetes of the Qur'an. They commented on each verse of the Qur'an. Most contemporary Muslim scholars cannot be called exegetes in the same way, yet they invariably return to the Qur'an because it continues to be the central text in Islamic intellectual thought and piety. One has only to look at different Muslim cultures around the world, to perceive the diversity of religious expression even though the Qur'an remains a unifying force among Muslims.

651/652 CE

Uthmanic codex

1300–73

Age of Ismail Ibn Kathir, one of the most influential Sunni Qur'an scholars

Sura al-Alaq (The Clot) the 96th sura in the Qur'an

the Qur'an began formally during the lifetime of the third successor, (caliph) Uthman ibn Affan (d. 656 CE).

THE OFFICAL QUR'AN

Uthman wanted to create the official text of the Qur'an and commissioned the Medinan Zayd ibn Thabit, one of Muhammad's scribes, to collate an official written version of the work. This event marks the canonization of the work.

For Muslims, within 20 years of Muhammad's death, the final collection of the Qur'an was established – that is, the 'book' came into being as a defined corpus of writing. Known as the 'Uthmanic codex', this is the book that was used as the model on which ultimately all subsequent copies were made and distributed throughout the lands and regions that gradually came under the expanding Muslim rule.

Scholars have claimed that, on the basis of the earliest manuscripts, which date from the ninth century, it took almost two centuries for the 'Uthmanic codex' to be accepted as the exclusive authority and affirmed as a 'correct' reading of the Qur'an. Only then did it become the model for all Qur'ans. Nevertheless, the Arabic text has remained remarkably uniform in all extant editions from the time of the 'Uthmanic codex' onwards. For many Muslims, this is itself a sign of the miracle of the Qur'an and its historical preservation is seen as sign of divine intervention itself.

CHAPTER AND VERSE

The Qur'an is a short book, consisting of 114 chapters called *suras*, arranged roughly in order of length from the longest to the shortest. These *suras* are divided into verses (*ayat*). The only exception to this ordering of *suras* is the first *sura*, which is called The Opening (*al-Fatiha*). This *sura* is recited daily by Muslims in ritual prayer.

Most of the *suras* have a name at the beginning, referring to a subject matter in that particular *sura*. With the exception of chapter 9 (Repentance), each *sura* begins with the phrase, *basmala* – in the name of God, the merciful, the compassionate. Despite covering all kinds of worldly and eschatological themes, the Qur'an is neither a book of law nor one of theology, but it is revered as a source for moral guidance.

> SAY, 'O MY SERVANTS WHO HAVE TRANSGRESSED, DO NOT DESPAIR OF THE MERCY OF GOD. INDEED, GOD FORGIVES ALL SINS. INDEED, IT IS HE WHO IS THE FORGIVING, THE MERCIFUL.
>
> Q39:53

THE VOICE OF GOD

While scholarly debates about the history, canonization, contextualization and diverse hermeneutical approaches to the Qur'an, occupy the minds of scholars, for Muslims, God is the author of the Qur'an. This is because he speaks through the Qur'an as its author, 'It is indeed We who have sent down the Qur'an and it is We who will protect it' (Q15:9). The Qur'an is a God-centred text; the 'I' or 'we' in the Qur'an is God speaking. God is lord, God is Creator and God is the most merciful. Through the act of creation, God expresses all three of these attributes. The various themes of God, prophets, salvation and the afterlife are inextricably intertwined in a book that is read and understood as a 'guide to man', complete in beauty and wisdom, claiming as the central tenet of the faith, the unicity of God (*tawhid*).

The Qur'an is not only meant to be read, but also heard and experienced as an object of devotion and spiritual power. Even though translations of the Qur'an are now available in most major languages, the Qur'an continues to be read and recited in Arabic by Muslims everywhere, because reading the Arabic of the Qur'an is understood to incur blessings on the believer.

The condensed idea
God himself is speaking through the Qur'an

35 Hadith and sunna

In Islam, the Prophet Muhammad is the final prophet and the recipient of God's final message, the Qur'an. For Muslims, Muhammad came to represent the greatest of humanity. It is for this reason that the reported sayings of the Prophet and his companions, known collectively as *hadiths*, are cited, memorized and revered by Muslims as much as the Qur'an itself. The *hadith* reports form part of the broader Prophetic example known as the *sunna*, which refers to the entirety of the Prophet's practices, customs and habits.

The word *hadith* originally meant a report and *sunna* the living tradition of a community rather than the example of the Prophet. However, both words ultimately became associated with the Prophet, ensuring their place in the Islamic legal tradition. With the exception of a limited number of verses in the Qur'an, the earliest Muslim literature dealing with legal matters are the *hadiths*. The bulk of Islamic law and practice does not come from the Qur'an. The Qur'an frequently commands believers to pray, and yet the precise instructions of how the prayer is performed, and at what times, is sourced only from the *hadiths* and *sunna*.

HADITH COLLECTIONS

Hadiths are long or short reports on a wide range of subjects – from what Muhammad said or did in his battles with Meccans, to relations with people of other faiths, relations with his wives, engaging in business and, of

632 CE	**8TH CENTURY CE**	**9TH CENTURY CE**
Prophet dies and the task of preserving his legacy begins	Muhammad ibn Ishaq writes an important biography of the Prophet	Collection of *hadith* canons by Muslim and Bukhari

course, issues of piety and devotion to God. Everything that touched Muhammad's life and the society in which he lived is represented. For many Muslims, the *hadiths* are the lens through which they approach and understand the Qur'an. There is also a group of *hadiths* known as *hadith qudsi*, which are understood to be words spoken by Muhammad under divine inspiration – that is, they are not wholly divine in the way that the Qur'an is, nor wholly prophetic in the way that ordinary *hadiths* are, but lie somewhere in between.

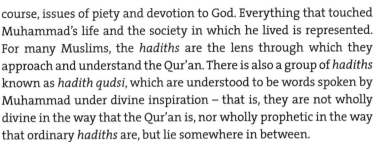

NONE OF YOU TRULY BELIEVES UNTIL HE LOVES FOR HIS BROTHER THAT WHICH HE LOVES FOR HIMSELF.
Bukhari and Muslim

While Sunni and Shi`a schools refer to their own *hadith* collections – which occasionally overlap – the basic structure of a *hadith* is the same. A report consists of a chain of narrators (*isnad*). The *isnad* is an attempt to demonstrate that the report is an accurate account of the events described, whether it goes back to a companion or to the Prophet himself. In theory, the list of names in the chain of transmitters acts as a guarantee that the text of the report (*matn*) is genuine. A typical *hadith* narration reads as follows:

> Al-Bukhari reported that: Yahya ibn Bukayr narrated to us from Al-Layth fromUqayl from Ibn Qadi Shuhba from`Urwah from `A'ishah, who said, 'Whenever the Prophet was given an option between two things, he used to select the easier of the two as long as it was not sinful; but if it was sinful, he would remain far from it'.

UNRELIABLE SOURCES

Hadiths initially spread orally in the immediate generations following the Prophet's death. But according to many Muslims, the *isnad* process could not guarantee authenticity, because it became subject to a great deal of fabrication. The challenge confronting Muslim scholars therefore lay in discerning what the Prophet had really said or done from the mass of fabricated *hadiths* that advanced particular religious or legal positions in

13TH CENTURY	**20TH CENTURY**
Imam an-Nawawi compiles his highly popular 'Forty *Hadith* Qudsi'	Rise of Western criticism of the authenticity of much of the *hadith* literature

The beauty of *hadith qudsi*

Imam Nawawi's *Forty Hadith* and *Forty Hadith Qudsi* are widely regarded as the most popular and most beautiful anthologies of the Prophet's sayings in the English language. They have been widely translated and reflect a particular kind of Islamic spirituality. One of the most eloquent is, 'My servant continues to draw near to me with supererogatory deeds until I love him. When I love him, I am his hearing with which he hears, and his sight with which he sees, and his hand with which he strikes, and his foot with which he walks. Were he to ask [something] of Me, I would surely give it to him; and were he to seek refuge with Me, I would surely grant him refuge.'

Another is that God has said, 'O Son of Adam, as long as you invoke me and ask of me, I shall forgive you for what you have done, and I shall not mind. O son of Adam, were your sins to reach the clouds of the sky and you then asked forgiveness from me, I would forgive you. O son of Adam, were you to come to me with sins nearly as great as the Earth, and were you then to face me, ascribing no partner to me, I would bring you forgiveness nearly as great as it.' Both *hadiths* can be accessed from the online site sunnah.com.

his name. Thus, a complex science of *hadith* developed, which aimed to separate weak examples from those that are considered sound (*sahih*). The ability to discern a reliable *hadith* from the many weak, and indeed forged, examples that came into circulation, was a meticulous exercise, and was regarded as a pinnacle of the pursuit of knowledge. This activity reached its zenith during the ninth century in the works of Muhammad ibn Ismail al-Bukhari (d. 870 CE) and Muslim ibn al-Hajjaj (d. 875 CE). Their collections of *hadiths* are regarded as the most authoritative compilations and are widely used by Muslims. As *hadiths* and *sunna* gradually became a source of law – second only to the Qur'an – Muhammad's purported behaviour became the central legal grounding for much of Islamic law.

COLLECTING HADITHS

Al-Bukhari and Muslim journeyed across the Islamic world, analyzing the mass of *hadiths* in circulation. This analysis involved rigorous investigation of the personal histories, characters and memory capacities of each figure involved in each stage of the transmission of a single *hadith*. It is said that al-Bukhari alone encountered more than 300,000 *hadith* narrations in his travels, from which only slightly over 6,000 were included in his collection, named the *Sahih al-Bukhari* – an acceptance rate of roughly two per cent.

Even within these various collections, *hadiths* were accorded the following levels of authenticity: frequently attested (*mutawatir*); authentic/sound (*sahih*), good (*hasan*) and weak (*da'if*). With the emergence of different legal and theological schools in medieval Islam, the status afforded *hadiths* often served a key point of difference and self-definition. Mu`tazilite thinkers triumphed the arbiter of human reason, and thus discounted those *hadiths* that appeared contradictory to rational proof. The conservative Hanbali school of law placed a strong emphasis on the literal, clear reading of the *hadith* text. The group's founder, Ahmad ibn Hanbal (d. 855 ce), famously declared he would rather follow even a weak *hadith* than his own reason.

THE HADITH IN MODERN TIMES

The place and relevance of many *hadiths* in contemporary societies poses a particular challenge. Knowledge and recitation of *hadiths* has grown in Muslim popular piety as an ongoing reflection of devotion to the Prophet. But to simply say 'the Prophet did such and such a thing' with little or no concern for either spirit, interpretation or context, is a challenge facing Muslims. What does one do, for example, with the *hadith* that records the Prophet ordering his community to kill any apostate, or those detailing the very early age of the Prophet's wife Aisha, at both marriage and consummation? There is no uniform way of negotiating these issues.

Among various responses is that of the 'Qur'an Only' movement, which rejects the authenticity of the *hadith* traditions, seeking instead to derive Muslim laws and ethics from the Qur'an alone. However, this remains a distinctly marginal movement in Islamic thought. To remove the *hadith* corpus not only dismantles key pillars of Muslim practice, but also disregards many other *hadiths* that speak movingly of God's justice and compassion, or that offer precious insights into the life and character of the Prophet.

The condensed idea
Hadiths are a daily part of Islamic piety

36 Sharia law

No other word alarms people in the West as much as that of 'sharia', loosely translated as 'Islamic law'. Yet the word *shari`a* occurs very seldom in its meaning as law and only once in the Qur'an, 'We put you, [O Muhammad], on an ordained way so follow it'. The word *shari`a* here designates a way or path that has been divinely appointed.

The word *shari`a* has a history among Jewish and Christian communities prior to its usage in Islam. The translation of the Old Testament into Arabic attributed to Saadia Gaon (d. 933) shows that *shari`a* was used by the Arabic-speaking Jewish community. The most commonly used term for translating Hebrew *torah* is Arabic *shari`a* or its plural. The word *shari`a* is also used to designate single rules or a system of rules in the Hebrew Bible. Around the tenth century, we also have the word *shari`a* in certain Christian writings, where the Christian religion, the law of the Messiah is referred to as *Shari`at al-Masih*. In Islamic literature, sharia and its various cognates also refer to a rule of law, laws or the totality of a particular prophetic message.

JURISPRUDENCE

Most Muslims use *shari`a* to mean God's law; sharia is the transcendent moral law of God, known only to God. Laws that are accessible to humans are referred to as *fiqh*, and are based on the elaborate interpretative works of the scholar jurists called the *fuqaha*. In other words, sharia is divine in origin, while *fiqh* – which means 'understanding' or 'jurisprudence' – is always a human activity. Although the concept of God's ideal law is

TIMELINE

796–855 CE	7TH–13TH CENTURY
Emergence of the great legal scholars Malik ibn Anas, Abu Hanifa, Al-Shafi`i and Ibn Hanbal	Various legal concepts and institutions define different versions of sharia

encapsulated in the word *shari`a*, it was the juristic discipline of *fiqh* that came to dominate the intellectual world of Islam. Jurisprudence was the most prestigious branch of Islamic sciences, valued more highly than theology or philosophy, despite some overlap. This was the situation right up until the period of European colonialism, after which European legal codes combined with aspects of sharia. From the end of the 19th century, however, in most Muslim countries, Islamic law was relegated largely to family law, including inheritance.

Fiqh was never more than a human approximation of a sacred ideal, a product that was ultimately a pious, but imperfect, effort. Its stylistic features combined juristic speculation with literary ingenuity.

SCHOOLS OF LAW

While there were several schools of law in early Sunni Islam, the groupings of these jurists eventually settled out at four schools (*maddhabs*). According to medieval Islam, these schools were named after their founders: Malik ibn Anas (d. 796), Abu Hanifa (d. 767), Al-Shafi`I (d. 822), and Ibn Hanbal (d. 855). Many Western scholars have argued that the founders of the schools were not responsible for establishing the 'schools' named after them, for example, Hanafi, Maliki, Shafi`i and Hanbali, but that it was the pupils of the founders who established the basic elements of the school. There are also Shi`i schools – the Zaydis and Ithna `Asharis – which developed separately.

As the four schools became established, jurists of individual schools wrote according to the methods and disciplines of that particular school, despite spatial and temporal differences. There were two ways by which the views

> **TO EACH OF YOU WE PRESCRIBED A LAW AND A METHOD. HAD GOD WILLED, HE WOULD HAVE MADE YOU ONE NATION, BUT HE INTENDED TO TEST YOU IN WHAT HE HAS GIVEN YOU. SO RACE TO ALL THAT IS GOOD. TO GOD IS YOUR RETURN ALL TOGETHER, AND HE WILL THEN INFORM YOU CONCERNING THAT OVER WHICH YOU USED TO DIFFER.**
> Q5:48

19TH CENTURY

Introduction of Western colonial legal systems into Muslim lands

2016

Home Office announces an independent commission to look at the place of sharia councils in the UK

Law and ethics

Over the last two decades, many Muslim scholars have focused attention on the historically prescriptive nature of Islamic law and how much of this tradition can continue to be valued as normative law in any real sense. The lament among some scholars, such as Fazlur Rahman Malik, is that if sharia is positive law, it is not always consistent with the ethical and moral imperatives of the Qur'an itself. There are those who claim that, in regarding the classical heritage as an immutable body of law, Muslims have ignored the essence of Islamic law in society – that is, whether in application or content, it was always changing with respect to social contexts. They argue that even where modifications have been made, or laws have been subsumed within post-colonial Western legal codes, the Muslim world has tied itself to conceptualizing human relations within a largely medieval framework. Others claim that these juristic works are the repository of pious reflection by men who had interpreted the fundamental sources of Islam; they contain within them the resources necessary for a re-thinking of social and legal attitudes and the revision of Islamic societies.

of different writers from different eras were established. One was through the exploration of those problems that each generation of jurists inherited from their ancestors and the other was through the process of citing past authorities.

The richness of juristic speculation within each school and across schools is contained in the diversity of juristic opinion (*ikhtilaf*), the central stylistic feature of *fiqh*. The principle of *ikhtilaf* allowed the jurists to put forward various perspectives on a single point of principle by the discussion of options and circumstances. As *fiqh* literature grew, these principles often became buried under the mound of detail and formula, but never lost the element of discussion and debate.

Sunni Islam recognizes four sources through which Islamic law is derived. These are the Qur'an, the *sunna* of the Prophet, the consensus (*ijma`*) of the community and analogical reasoning (*qiyas*). Islamic law is divided between works of positive law (*furu`*) and the principles of law *(usul)*. A fundamental hermeneutical aspect of *furu`* is *ijtihad*, meaning 'effort'. Technically it refers to the individual effort made by each jurist to take into account all principles of interpretation to discover a rule of law.

Those who exercised *ijtihad* became known as *mujtahids*. A *mujtahid* who was asked a direct question was known as a *mufti* and his legal opinion is known as a *fatwa*. From the ninth to the tenth centuries, major works of positive law have largely covered the same topics and have a similar structure. As well as exploring areas of worship, such as purity, prayer and fasting, topics include marriage, divorce, inheritance laws, sale and penal laws. All areas of life are subject to moral and legal reflection.

CRIMES AGAINST GOD

Most non-Muslims, however, equate sharia with the fixed penalties known as *hudud*. In classical law, these are known as crimes against God, mentioned either in the Qur'an or the *hadiths*. The crimes are unlawful intercourse, false accusation of unlawful intercourse, drinking wine, theft, armed robbery and, in most schools, apostasy. For these crimes, there are fixed penalties, involving a mixture of flogging, amputation or even death.

Strict rules of evidence and complex nuances on what counted as a crime, made application of the penalties very difficult to carry out. During the 19th century, many Muslim countries abolished Islamic criminal law completely and replaced it with Western statute law. While some Muslim majority societies continue to practise these punishments, or threaten their use, many reformers, scholars and human rights activists in the Islamic world argue that they should be abolished completely, as they were never meant to be immutable and are used only as a means of oppressing society; they go against the ethical and interpretative spirit of Islamic law.

Thinking the unthought

Thinkers, writers, artists, scholars and economic producers must all be committed to injecting new dynamism into Muslim ethics. Thoughts have their own life force and no dominating ideology can encapsulate the richness of Islam. We need the freedom to think the unthought, as the late Mohammed Arkoun said, because otherwise we remain intellectually and emotionally trapped in fear.

The condensed idea
Sharia is belief, law, ritual and guidance

37 Islamic law and the West

It is very difficult to generalize as to the extent that sharia is applied in Muslim majority or Muslim minority countries today. Yet sharia still resonates with Muslims, because it implies the totality of a pious life, not just the simplistic attitudes to criminal law and punishment.

slamic law is used as the most common translation of the word *shari`a*, which in itself is the umbrella term used to signify all aspects of religious and cultural legalism in Muslim societies; that which is sharia, is God's law. This perception is fortified by an increasing predilection in popular Islamic piety to be dogmatic about sharia, with little awareness of the nuanced interpretation and diversity that is an essential aspect of legal literature. If anything, Muslim discourse around sharia has, in current times, used the term as a simplistic mark of distinct ritual and political identity.

REVIEWING SHARIA LAW

There is no one sharia, and over the centuries Islamic law has been interpreted and applied in a range of ways. Yet with the rise of violent extremism and certain Muslim states and militant groups calling for a return to sharia law, Islamic law is often seen as criminal law only and reduced to punishments of lashings or stoning. It means that anyone calling for a more nuanced understanding of the application of religious law in the West is met with a certain hostility.

TIMELINE

1960s	1980s
Jabir al-Alwani found *fiqh al-aqalliyyat* (Muslim minority jurisprudence) in the US	Sharia councils set up in the UK

This happened in 2008 when the then Archbishop of Canterbury, Dr Rowan Williams, delivered the Foundation Lecture for the Temple Church at the Royal Courts of Justice on 7 February 2008 entitled, 'Islam in English Law'. Both his lecture and the earlier BBC radio discussion provoked a blistering backlash against the primate from an array of political and religious voices. To hear the leader of the Anglican Church call for any sort of 'constructive accommodation' of Muslim practice rather than proclaim a more robust vision of Christianity, was more than most could tolerate.

IN CIVILIZED LIFE, LAWS FLOAT IN A SEA OF ETHICS.

Earl Warren (1891–1974)

The problem, however, lies not in the existence of religious law but in the nebulous status of certain aspects of religious culture. Sharia as worship is part of the Muslim migration story in the West. The prohibition on pork, abstention from alcohol, five-times ritual prayers and fasting in Ramadan are all aspects of sharia. When observed, no violation of the civil law takes place. In the area of personal law, most Muslims marry according to their religious law and register their marriage under the civil law of the land. For decades the two systems have existed side by side and there is nothing here that contradicts the laws of most Western countries.

ARBITRATION TRIBUNALS

In September 2008, however, sharia courts became classified as arbitration tribunals, taking advantage of a clause in the Arbitration Act 1996. Jewish Beth Din courts have operated under the same provision in the Arbitration Act for over 100 years whereby they have been able to resolve civil cases and issues relating to personal law. Now, Muslim arbitration tribunals can give rulings that are binding in law, provided that both parties in the dispute agree to give the tribunal the power to rule on their case. On criminal matters, the laws of the United Kingdom prevail and sharia courts have no jurisdiction

2005

7/7 bombings on London's transport system

2008

Rowan Williams lectures on Islam in English Law at the Royal Courts of Justice.

Terrorism changed everything

It would be no exaggeration to say that, despite a general awareness of sharia as Islamic law, for most non-Muslims in the UK, sharia was quite simply a foreign word with a foreign meaning. This changed after the London bombings in July 2005.

Counterterrorism police operations were suddenly plunged into multiple cases of suspected bomb plots, cases in which the written material they found was full of words and theological concepts that had little or no meaning for them. Words such as *kafir* and jihad featured frequently in the literature discovered in many of the suspects' homes.

While many in the police and security forces came to grips with some of the more general vocabulary, it was soon apparent that an in-depth knowledge of Islamic sources was fundamental to any successful operation and, where applicable, subsequent conviction. The terrorists were using theological sources and much of this was incomprehensible to many in the security services.

This matter has been further complicated by the S2 Terrorism Act 2006, which creates offences relating to the sale and other dissemination of books and other publications – including material on the Internet – that encourages people to engage in terrorism, or that provides information that could be useful to terrorism.

Many scholars have been approached to help as expert witnesses – people who can shed light on some of the more complex arguments of classical Islamic law, especially in the area of military jihad.

on these matters. However, several politicians and public figures have raised concern over this recognition, quite simply because there is not much awareness as to which courts are enforcing the rulings made by the arbitration tribunals.

Furthermore, while these courts insist that they recognize the limits of arbitration councils, and that they have no wish to set up any parallel jurisdiction, many are concerned that they may ignore a fundamental principle; except for matters of personal conscience, sharia law must always be subsidiary to the laws of the state.

GREY AREAS

Where there exist abusive practices within Muslim cultures, how does English law differentiate between sharia as valid practice from sharia as illegal? For example, if arranged marriages are premised on adult consent, forced marriages ignore this premise, ignoring individual consent. Many in the legal profession are aware that Islamic divorce proceedings must be done within the framework of both religious and civil law. However, they are also aware of the dangerous position in which this leaves women who become victims caught between two legal systems. An increasing number of family and criminal cases involving Muslims are coming to the British courts. These include issues of marriage and divorce, but also crimes such as honour killings. It is not surprising, therefore, that some people express genuine concern about the place of sharia in the West and see it only as a negative or oppressive system.

A NEW INTERPRETATION

It would seem that while Europe as a whole is coming to terms with the cultural realities of Islam, Islamism and Islamic law, it remains suspicious of what sharia might actually mean. Many Muslims are keen to keep their personal understanding of sharia pertinent in all aspects of private and public life. Islamic law as a political system may be defunct, but Islamic law as part of ritual, worship and moral guidance still functions.

The claim is that, in general, Muslim attitudes to sharia have been hugely varied and the nature and validity of many aspects of Islamic law have been contested. However, the principles that lay behind the formulation of law can still be applied today, to develop new thinking that would be in line with more contemporary notions and standards of human dignity and universal principles of human freedom.

The condensed idea
Sharia means more than punishments

38 The mosque

A place of worship, learning and community, the mosque (*masjid*) is the focal point of the Muslim community. Images of beautiful domes and soaring minarets have become the definitive emblem of Islamic civilization.

The Arabic term for 'mosque' is *masjid*, literally meaning a 'place of prostration' (*sujud*). The most famous mosque in the Muslim world is *al-masjid al-haram* ('the sacred mosque') situated around the Kaaba in Mecca (see Chapter 6). This is referred to 15 times in the Qur'an. Also of great significance is the *al-masjid al-nabawi*, or 'Prophet's Mosque', located in Medina. This is the site of the Prophet's house upon his emigration to Medina, and marks the first mosque of the new religious community.

ARCHITECTURAL FEATURES

The Qur'an gives no specific instructions on what form a mosque should take, and this is reflected in the broad variety of architectural designs seen around the Islamic world. The stunning beauty of many mosques means they are often considered among the finest examples of architecture, with their range of styles reflecting the diverse cultures and traditions of the Islamic world. In general, however, there are several key features that are central to all mosques.

The main area of a mosque comprises the prayer hall, in which believers congregate and perform the main prayers. Within the prayer hall is the *minbar,* which dates back to the time of the Prophet and is a short set of stairs leading to a pulpit, from where the imam addresses the congregation

TIMELINE

711 CE	970 CE	1453
Muslims capture Spain	Al-Azhar Mosque built in Cairo	Fall of Constantinople

during the communal Friday prayer service. In many mosques, alongside the *minbar* is be the *mihrab*: a semi-circular niche carved into the wall, indicating the direction to Mecca. The *mihrab* is often adorned with intricate designs and Arabic calligraphy.

> **SO WORSHIP ME AND ESTABLISH PRAYER FOR MY REMEMBRANCE.**
>
> Q20:14

INTERIOR DESIGN

The interior designs of mosques vary greatly, reflecting both cultural and theological differences. Some mosques are furnished with lavish decorations and ornate calligraphy of Qur'anic verses or the names of God. Other mosques, particularly in the Arabian context, are more austere, shunning excessive decoration as a distraction from the main focus of worshipping God. Throughout all mosques the use of religious imagery is rejected. Perhaps the most defining feature of the mosque is the minaret: a tall, slender tower usually found adjacent to the main building. It is from the minaret that the call to prayer is sent in Muslim-majority countries.

CENTRES OF LEARNING AND COMMUNITY

In classical Islamic civilization, the mosque played a pivotal role in the spread of education. The great mosques of cities that include Baghdad, Cairo, Istanbul and Damascus were known primarily as centres of learning. Students would travel from across the Islamic world to learn from renowned teachers in the mosque – both in the field of religious disciplines like Qur'an and *hadith* studies, but also broader fields such as chemistry, astrology, mathematics and logic.

Today, mosques have largely lost this educative function, yet they remain more than simply places of prayer. Particularly in the West, many mosques perform the role of a traditional community centre. Many mosques provide evening classes in Arabic and Islamic studies, establish social circles for women, children or converts, organize charitable events and assist with

1889

First mosque built in the UK, the Shah Jahan Mosque in Woking

1981

Saudi government enlarges Prophet's mosque to five times original size

From church to mosque

One of the most significant consequences of the spread of Islam and Christianity throughout history is that mosques have been converted into churches and churches into mosques. One of the greatest architectural examples is the Hagia Sophia in Istanbul (formerly Constantinople). The Hagia Sophia (see below), known also as the Church of the Holy Wisdom, was a cathedral built at Constantinople in the sixth century (535 CE) under the Byzantine emperor, Justinian 1. It is considered to be one of the world's greatest Byzantine structures. In 1453, Constantinople was captured by the Ottoman Turks under Sultan Mehmet II, who ordered that this church of orthodox Christianity be converted into a mosque. It remained a mosque until 1931 when it was secularized and opened as a museum on 1 February 1935 by the Republic of Turkey.

marital difficulties, among other activities. Some have become centres for voter registration during election campaigns, or operate as 'third-party reporting' sites in liaison with the police. In larger mosques it is common to find libraries and other social facilities, such as gymnasiums.

GENDER SEGREGATION

There is no mention in the Qur'an of any gender segregation for male and female believers inside the mosque. However, during the time of the Prophet and throughout Muslim tradition, Muslim women would pray in the back rows of the main prayer hall, behind the men. This does not reflect theological superiority, but stems from more practical concerns. The specific postures and movements of prayer, such as bending before prostration, are seen as potentially uncomfortable for women, and distracting for men, were women to be placed at the front.

Today, the issue of gender segregation has attracted controversy. In recent years it has become common in many mosques, including those in the West, for female worshippers to pray behind a partition, visibly out of sight. Many mosques in the West have no room for female worshippers at all. This is often justified by a lack of space in many converted mosques, and the fact that, while the Friday congregational prayer is obligatory for Muslim men, it is merely recommended for women. However, this does not silence accusations that Islamic gender segregation has lead to a culture of gender exclusion across many Muslim communities.

THE MOSQUE IN THE WEST

The construction of large mosques in major European cities, such as London, Paris and Moscow, is perhaps the clearest symbol of Muslim presence in Europe, and is not without controversy. Plans to build mosques in British cities have been challenged and, in rare cases, mosques have been vandalized. In these cases, it is not the construction of a house of worship that unsettles, but the perceived difference in ideas and values that a mosque represents. Today, some mosques are targets for surveillance, but while suspicions remain, some claim that minarets and domes in Western cities reflect the success of religious freedom and cultural diversity in the West.

From mosque to church

The mosque-cathedral of Cordoba is one of the greatest architectural legacies of Moorish Spain. When Muslims conquered Spain in 711 CE, the Catholic church built to honour St Vincent III is said to have been divided into Muslim and Christian halves. This shared arrangement lasted until 784 CE, when the Christian half was purchased by the Muslim ruler `Abd al-Rahman I, who demolished the original structure and built the Grand Mosque of Cordoba on its grounds. Cordoba returned to Christian rule in 1236 during the Reconquista and the building became a Roman Catholic church. A Renaissance cathedral nave was added during the 16th century. Muslims can no longer pray in this cathedral. The building is most notable for its arcaded hall, double arches amd 856 columns of onyx, marble and granite that are made from pieces from a Roman temple.

The condensed idea
No building can contain God

39 The madrasa

The foremost educational institution of medieval Islam was the madrasa. The word comes from the root meaning 'to learn or study' and the simplest definition of *madrasa* is 'school' or 'place of learning'. While madrasas have been part of the Islamic landscape for centuries, today in the West, a madrasa has assumed a new significance as a place that could promote religious extremism.

Sunni Islam was never organized around clerical elites or religious hierarchies. There were no authorities like councils or synods, nor any equivalent of bishops and cardinals to debate the question as to what constituted theological orthodoxy. Sunni Islam instead centred on the mosque. It was the mosque that grew from humble beginnings to become a place of learning along with the madrasa, which served not only as a place for religious education, but also for non-religious curricula, including Arabic grammar and the sciences. Some people have compared the madrasa to a seminary for Christian students.

THE ADVENT OF THE MADRASA

In the early period of Islam, mosques served as places of learning in which scholars met with circles of students. But as the Muslim Empire expanded and grew more complex, new institutions dedicated to teaching and learning emerged, in the form of madrasas. Some contemporary scholars have claimed that the informality of the relationship between teacher

TIMELINE

970 CE	1227
Al-Azhar University established in Cairo, one of the first universities in the world	Famous al-Mustan-siriya madrasa established in Baghdad

and student in the premodern Islamic educational system remained the central feature of learning in the madrasas. It has also been claimed that the premodern madrasa grew rapidly as an institution, in part because of the generous patronage of wealthy individuals who created charitable trusts (*waqf/awqaf*) to found educational institutions. This may have given some of them a level of independence from the ruling authorities but it did not stop people such as the vizier Nizam al-Mulk endowing some of the most illustrious colleges of the day such as the Nizamiyya madrasa, in which the famous theologian/jurist al-Ghazali taught for many years.

> ❝ ONE WHO TREADS A PATH IN SEARCH OF KNOWLEDGE HAS HIS PATH TO PARADISE MADE EASY BY GOD. ❞
> *Hadith*

A GOLDEN AGE

The Seljuq period, from the 11th to the 13th centuries, is generally considered the time at which madrasas became the main institutions for the preservation and transmission of knowledge – notably the expansion of Sunni Islam into the broader culture. By the 11th century, the madrasa was established as a complex of buildings with dormitories for students, libraries and even hospitals. They were devoted primarily to the religious sciences such as Qur'an interpretation, *hadith* studies and, perhaps most importantly, jurisprudence. It was the jurists who defined orthodox religion through their reflection on details of the law. Sharia education was the dominant form of education and the dominant profession within the religious elite.

By the early 13th century there were several madrasas in Baghdad, the most famous being the al-Mustansiriya, named after the caliph Al-Mustansir (1226–42). It housed all four Sunni legal schools and its library was reputed to have an initial collection of some 80,000 books, donated by the caliph.

1866

Deoband Darul Ulum madrasa established in Deoband, India

2015

UK Government announces plans to regulate and inspect Britain's 2,000 madrasas

Who do scholars write for?

An interesting question about the Islamic intellectual tradition is, who were the scholars of the formative and classical period writing for? Maybe this is a very modern question and we may never really know why they wrote or how their efforts were received.

Modern understanding of scholarship is largely a Western understanding of scholarship, which enquires after originality, sources and influence. More often than not, the modern audience is assumed to be secular and liberal, rather than confessional or literalist. Knowledge is not related to religious piety in the same way. Furthermore, how did early Muslims teach and educate?

Since the 1980s, there has been much progress regarding the question of oral and written transmission of knowledge in early Islam – that is, in the first three centuries of the religion. The scholarly sessions (*majalis*) held by Muslim scholars for the purpose of teaching their students, relied largely on oral instruction. Written material in the form of collections of data and 'lecture scripts' were used as memory aids and it is quite possible that over the course of time, these collections came to be fixed in memory and writing.

But the concept of a book did not gain shape in early Muslim scholarship, although scholars exercised authorial creativity through their selection of themes and displayed a sophisticated method of internal referencing in various written forms. Written collections were used and absorbed by subsequent generations of Muslims.

The Ottomans were also great builders of madrasas, and the first Ottoman madrasa was built in Iznik in 1331. Most madrasas were built around mosques in important cities, such as Baghdad, Damascus and Cairo. They were built of stone with fine architecture and decorated with carvings and tiles.

LEADING SCHOOLS

In India and Pakistan, Sunni madrasas are often divided between the Deobandi and Barelvi schools of thought. The Deobandi movement's intellectual and spiritual heart is in the Indian city of Deoband. Its Darul Uloom Deoband is reputed to be the second largest madrasa in the Sunni Muslim world, following only by Al-Azhar madrasa in Cairo.

The Deobandi movement began with the founding of the Darul Uloom Deoband in 1866 in reaction to British colonialism and English-language education in India. While the Darul Uloom remains a respected organization in the Muslim world, it faces criticism for being too socially conservative and hard-lined in many of its views, having been influenced by the Wahhabi movement. The Barelvi movement is distinct by being more diffuse and also conforming to many Sufi practices.

The Deobandi–Barelvi sectarian influence can be seen in madrasas in the West. Today, in the West, madrasas offer a supplementary religious education outside of the mainstream school system. Hundreds of madrasas exist, and while many teach Qur'an recitation and the fundamentals of the Islamic faith, there is no agreed and uniform curriculum. Some government ministers have, in recent years, expressed concern at the relative lack of rigorous regulation and fear that these institutions may be teaching extremist ideologies to young people. Accordingly, various initiatives have been put in place, including that of providing citizenship lessons.

The condensed idea
Madrasas can be places of worship and learning

40 Salafism

There is no unanimously agreed understanding of Salafism. In its broadest sense, the term 'salafi Islam' denotes an aspiration by modern Islamic movements that seek to reimagine Islamic societies by returning to the original scriptural sources of the Qur'an and Prophetic *sunna*. Salafism uses as its reference point the practices of the Prophet's companions and the first three centuries of Islam.

The term 'salafism' comes from the Arabic *as-salaf as-salih* meaning 'the righteous predecessors'. The Salafi movement emulates the practices of Muhammad and the early generations of Muslims, viewing this early era as a 'golden age' of Islam in which the pure, pristine version of the faith was practised. This is based upon the *hadith* in which Muhammad is reported to have said: 'The best of the people are my generation, then those after them, then those after them . . .' Salafism holds that this early faith became tainted by later cultural accretions and doctrinal innovations seeping into the religion. Much like the first Protestant reformers, therefore, Salafi Islam attempts to liberate the Qur'an and Prophetic *sunna* from the dead weight of Muslim tradition, and reconnect contemporary Muslims with their original sources. The focus is on a pure form of Islam, one stripped of centuries of accumulated theological and legal tradition.

MUSLIM TRADITION
Salafis take recourse to the legal and theological opinions of Shaykh al-Islam Ibn Taymiyya (d. 1328), even though Taymiyyah is not considered the

TIMELINE

622–661 CE	1263–1328
Period of the righteous salaf; the Prophet and 'rightly guided caliphs'	Life of Ibn Taymiyyah, key inspiration for Salafi movements today

progenitor of the Salafi movement. The 'Salafi' term today is a broad label, encompassing a wide variety of intellectual trends. The earliest form of Salafi Islam emerged in the late 19th and early 20th centuries, spearheaded by Muslim reformers Muhammad Abduh (d. 1905) and his student, Rashid Ridda (d. 1935). Responding to the cultural, political and scientific advances of the West, Muhammad Abduh sought to demonstrate the compatibility of Islam with the dominant Western values that were underpinning such progress. Abduh argued that Muslims had failed to match Western ascendancy owing to an excessive reliance on fossilized understandings of Islamic tradition and law, coupled with the failure to develop a culture of critical reasoning that was so prevalent in the West. These values were enshrined in the Qur'an, yet Muslims lost this impulse by their uncritical following and dependency upon the accumulated Muslim tradition. The famous quote, that has become a hallmark of this trend, is attributed to Abduh:

> *TODAY'S ISLAMIC FUNDAMENTALISM IS ALSO A COVER FOR POLITICAL MOTIFS. WE SHOULD NOT OVERLOOK THE POLITICAL MOTIFS WE ENCOUNTER IN FORMS OF RELIGIOUS FANATICISM.*
>
> Jürgen Habermas (b. 1929)

> I went to the West, and I saw Islam, but no Muslims; I got back to the East, and saw Muslims, but no Islam.

In recent decades this early form of Salafism has been largely supplanted by a more austere form of religious conservatism. The dominant Salafi trend today supports literal readings of the Qur'an, eschewing symbolic and metaphorical interpretations, and places a strong emphasis on the *hadith* traditions. Contemporary Salafi movements carry an emphasis on ritual observance, and stress the importance of following the dress, appearance and daily manners and customs of the Prophet. As a corollary to this, practices that are popular throughout many Islamic contexts, such as the visitation of graves, saint veneration and the use of religious icons, are rejected by Salafi Muslims as having no prophetic warrant and thus become an unlawful innovation (*bida'a*) in religion.

1932

Creation of the modern state of Saudi Arabia; global spread of localized 'Wahhabi' Salafism

2001–16

Salafi Islam increasingly linked with violent jihadi movements

Globalization and knowledge

One of the effects of globalization is that, in most Muslim societies, globalization has led to the erosion of traditional methods of knowledge production and dissemination. Mass communication and literacy have led to diverse ways of democratizing knowledge, even though the decentrality of knowledge has always been part of the Islamic world. The issue of authority and who speaks for Islam is tied to the various political movements that have emerged over the last 100 years. Charismatic figures are associated with various religio-political movements and what they all share, to some extent, is that religion does and should continue to play a role in Muslim societies. The perpetual backdrop of geopolitics in a globalized world serves instantly to politicize any articulation of an Islamic position on all kinds of matters and there is always a search for an authentic Islam on any events that occur in the Islamic world or that touches on Islam.

The phrase 'global Muslim politics' is often misleadingly used to insinuate that the vast majority of the world's 1.25 billion Muslims are strongly tied to any one or other social movement, doctrinal tendency or sharply defined ideological position. As a result 'extremist', 'moderate', 'liberal' and now 'radical' have become ways of referring to a 'Muslim position' on a variety of matters. Most Muslims find themselves being ascribed such labels even if they have no particular ties to any kind of political Islam or Islamic movement.

WAHHABISM

Today, this dominant trend of Salafi Islam has become very influential, and is possibly the fastest-growing movement in the Islamic world and among Muslim communities in the West. Reasons for this point to the role of Saudi Arabia, where there is a particular, localized form of Salafi Islam. Commonly referred to as Wahhabism, it is named after its eponym, Muhammad ibn Abdul al-Wahhab (d. 1792). Wahhab sought to purge the Arabian peninsula of what he considered to be the deviations of the popular religious practices in the region. This involved the destruction of many shrines and graves linked to the early companions of the Prophet as well as those of later Muslim saints. Today, with its oil exportation, the publication and translation of much Salafi-Wahhabi thought, and its religious significance as the guardian of the sacred sites of Mecca and Medina, Saudi Arabia has come to be seen by many as the largest exporter and propagator of this form of Islam.

At the same time, many Muslims are critical of the influence of Salafi movements. Many decry the perceived excessive importance given to matters of ritual and appearance at the expense of cultivating inner spirituality.

Other thinkers note the problem in returning to the era of the Prophet and his companions in the face of what are the intrinsically modern challenges facing Muslims today – notions of citizenship, secularism and nation-state democracy – issues that the Prophet and early communities would have never encountered. The Salafi movement is critiqued by these detractors for a perceived failure to appreciate the importance of these real, pressing issues.

MILITARIST TRENDS

The majority of groups championing Salafism are pacifist, yet there are minority voices within the movement who adopt a more militarist position, promoting a military jihad (see Chapter 47). The objective is usually to remove secular rulers from Muslim lands or to maintain a state of perpetual conflict against those non-Muslim governments who have militarily intervened in Muslim lands. Today, in the West, the label 'Salafi' is often associated with this strain of violent, jihadi extremism. Yet this is an oversimplification of the realities of contemporary Salafi movements. So-called 'Salafi-jihadi' groups, such as al-Qaeda and Islamic State differ from other Salafi movements, both in their engagement with political processes and in their use of indiscriminate violence. The majority of Salafi movements favour political quietism and non-involvement, seeing the state as a corrupting influence upon religion. Other groups engage with political processes, yet through legitimate, peaceful means. Moreover, these various strands often compete with each other, each claiming to adhere exclusively to the 'true' form of Salafism. The rise of a particularly violent, jihadist trend, epitomized by groups like Islamic State, therefore reflect as much an internal battle for religious authority and legitimacy within contemporary Salafi Islam itself, as it does an external battle between ideas of Islam and the West.

The condensed idea
There is always some movement to 'purify' Islam

41 Sufism

Sufism (*tasawwuf*) is the mystical-ascetic dimension of Islam. It is a practice that focuses on the inner dimensions of faith and spiritual transformation through a desire for closeness and intimacy with God. Over time, Sufi orders, practices and personalities have been instrumental in the spread of Islam in many parts of Asia and Africa.

The origins of the word *Sufi* lie in the eighth-century Islamic context for ascetics wearing woollen clothes and, possibly, also via a lexical root, denoting purity. The beginnings of Sufism come to us largely from tenth-century texts, which show that, for the early ascetics, the main source of inspiration was the Qur'an. In their eyes, the first Sufi was the Prophet himself. There was an emphasis on cultivating the perfect man, in the belief that becoming truly human is a journey in which the destination is a return to the unknowable one, God himself. However, while Sufism emphasized a level of asceticism, it saw itself very much within orthodox Islam, where observance of the law, prayers and the externals of the faith, were still seen as binding upon individuals.

BROTHERHOOD

The journey or spiritual path (*tariqa*) that also came to be known as 'brotherhood' or 'order' was a structured way of providing mystical guidance. There were several stations, each reflecting a gradual turning away from the material world and closeness to God. The 11th century Sufi al-Qushayri enumerates many stations, including such concepts as trust in God (*tawakkul*),

TIMELINE

8TH CENTURY CE	922 CE	1095–1105
Early ascetics known for wearing rough, woollen clothes (*sufi*)	Al-Hallaj executed for his claim 'I am the Truth'	Al-Ghazali goes into spiritual retreat; discovers the Sufi path

desire for God (*irada*), passionate longing for God (*shawq*) and mystic knowledge or gnosis (*marifah*). Central to Sufism was the practice of *dhikr*, or remembrance, which focused on mentioning God constantly through such phrases as the first part of the witness to faith, 'There is no god but God' (see Chapter 10).

> **WHAT HAS HE FOUND WHO HAS LOST GOD? AND WHAT HAS HE LOST WHO HAS FOUND GOD?**
>
> Ibn Ata Allah al-Iskandari
> (1259–1310)

Most Sufis saw this journey as one requiring a spiritual master and thus many aspirants attached themselves to a spiritual teacher. This master–disciple (*pir–murid*) relationship was the context in which groups emerged informally, with allegiance to a master or sheikh, and thus a link to a spiritual chain that would almost always go back to the Prophet. Lay Sufis who did not live in the Sufi lodges but worked in ordinary jobs also attended rituals and prayers regularly. Several *tariqas* existed in classical Islam, the most famous being the Suhrawardiyya, the Qadiriyya, the Mevlevi and the Naqshbandiyya. Not everyone who became a great spiritual leader set out to found an order and they were not exclusive – a Sufi could belong to several at once.

ASPECTS OF SUFISM

Certain names have come to define different aspects of Sufism. Al-Junayd (d. 910) is said to have elaborated the doctrine of *fana'* (absorption) into God, which is then followed by a return to the community to spread the word of God. His is commonly known as sober mysticism, in contrast with Bayazid al-Biastami (d. 875) who emphasized the importance of ecstasy or drunkenness (*sukr*) in one's love for God, rather than a focus on piety and obedience alone. Among the most famous of this order was al-Hallaj (d. 922) who was condemned to death for allegedly saying 'I am the Truth', which was understood to mean that he thought he was God incarnate.

Ibn al-`Arabi (d. 1240) was a great Spanish Sufi philosopher and poet who conceived of the Perfect Man (the Microcosm or *al-Insan al-Kamil*) as both

13TH CENTURY	**13TH–16TH CENTURIES**
Jalal al-Din Rumi writes his masterpiece, *Mathnawi*	'Golden age of Sufism' spreads to India

Sufi poetry and love of God

Sufis were inspired by the Qur'anic verses on God's love and mercy. For them the merciful God inspired Sufi poetry in which the Sufi is a lover desperately desiring some kind of relationship – even identification – with the beloved, God. Perhaps no Sufi has made this more manifest than the tenth-century Persian mystic Mansur al-Hallaj, who cried out 'I am the Truth' (*ana 'l-Haqq*). Some saw this as an act of blasphemy, a claim to divinity; others saw it as an annihilation of his ego, the ultimate destination for the mystic.

The ineffability of love is the focus of much of Rumi's poetry. The theme is immortalized in the lines, 'Love is most illumined by silence. When the pen was busy writing, it was fluent; when it reached the word of love, it broke down'. Despite being a universal experience, love remains indefinable. This line is testimony to the fact that the Qur'anic expressions of love and mercy inspired some of the most eloquent poetry. If the pen broke when it reached the word 'love' it is impossible to define God's love for humanity. Yet many Sufis see the whole of the cosmos as pulsating with the love that flows from God and the ecstasy of desiring God.

The execution of Mansur al-Hallaj

male and female. In his doctrine of the 'unity of being' (*wahdat al-wujud*), in which being and existence are all one combined in God, he emphasized the potential that *all* humans possess, to know of the oneness of God. His most famous works are 'The Bezels of Wisdom' and 'The Meccan Revelations'.

The most famous Sufi across the world today is Jalal al-Din Rumi (d. 1273), known in the Middle East as *Mawlana* (Turkish, *Mevlana*), meaning 'Our Lord'. While he wrote extensively, his magnum opus is the *Mathnawi*, a poem of 26,000 rhyming couplets that became popularly known as 'the Qur'an in Persian'. The Mevlevi Sufi order was founded in 1273 by Rumi's followers and the Mevlevi Sufis are also known as Whirling Dervishes who became famous for their whirling, spiritual dance. Rumi's work stressed the universal message of love in his own quest for nearness with God.

The whole hagiographical literature of Sufism throws up two particular tensions. One is that this kind of literature is given to a pious exaggeration of the various saints and their lives, with stories telling of all kinds of miracles. The second is that, at least until the medieval period, we are entirely dependent on the hagiographical record of male compilers. Yet women Sufis did achieve and receive recognition, albeit often measured by male standards. One of the best-known is the liberated slave girl of Basra, Rabi`a al-`Adawiyya (d. 801), whose writings and singular devotion transformed Sufism into an ecstatic love mysticism. Rabi`a had no time or interest in anyone other than God. She is the one whose haunting lines immortalized her consuming love of God, when she said that she wanted to love God for God alone, not out of fear of hell or desire for paradise.

SUFISM TODAY

Sufism continues to play an integral role in Muslim societies today – not to provide an alternative Islam, but to strengthen a person's faith and piety in his or her love for God. Religious poetry in the form of *qawwali* music, which relives the great saints' spiritual achievements, is played in many Islamic societies, especially in the Indian subcontinent. The tombs and shrines of legendary Sufis are also venerated as a focus for individual prayer. Orthodoxy has, at times, remained suspicious of Sufi practices, and some countries, such as Saudi Arabia, have banned saint adoration on the grounds that it verges on idolatry. But for many Muslim societies, the orders of the legendary Sufi masters and their disciples continue to invigorate the faith and provide cohesion within local cultures. This has been essential to gaining a wider, mystical perspective on the relations between believers and their faith.

The condensed idea
Sufism inspired the growth of Islam

42 Al-Ghazali

Abu Hamid Muhammad al-Ghazali is deemed by some to be the greatest ethical thinker in Islamic history. His contemporaries were in such admiration of his work that they gave him the honorific title, *hujjat al-Islam* or 'proof of Islam'. The notable jurist, al-Subki stated that 'if there had been a prophet after Muhammad, al-Ghazali would have been the man'.

Al-Ghazali was a jurist of the Shafi`i school, but he was also a philosopher, a theologian and a Sufi of Sunni Islam. In fact, he was a true polymath who excelled in whatever he turned his mind to. He is widely seen to be a renewer (*mujaddid*) in line with the well-known prophetic tradition that such a figure would arise every hundred years.

Born in around 1058 in Tabaran, in the district of Tus, some 24 km (15 miles) north of modern-day Mashhad in Iran, Ghazali was educated in his home town and went on to study with the influential Ash'arite theologian al-Juwaynî at the Nizâmiyya Madrasa in nearby Nishapur. The grand-vizier of the court, Nizam al-Mulk, appointed al-Ghazali to the prestigious Nizamiyya Madrasa in Baghdad, where he became closely connected to the court and was regarded the most influential intellectual of his time.

THE TRUE REALITY OF THINGS
In 1095, al-Ghazali grew frustrated with scholastic philosophy. Suffering a spiritual crisis, he gave up his teaching and left the city. Under the influence of Sufi mystical literature, he realized that virtuous acts predispose the soul

TIMELINE

1058	1091	1095
Al-Ghazali is born in Tus, modern-day Iran	Al-Ghazali is appointed to the prestigious Nizamiyya Madrasa in Baghdad	He suffers a spiritual crisis and undergoes a period of deep scepticism; leaves Baghdad

to receive God's grace – thinking that is located in the Qur'anic verse, 'The mercy of God is near to those who do good'.

NEVER HAVE I DEALT WITH ANYTHING MORE DIFFICULT THAN MY OWN SOUL, SOMETIMES IT HELPS ME AND SOMETIMES IT OPPOSES ME.

Al-Ghazali (d. 1111)

In his autobiography, *al-Munqidh min al-Dalal* (*Deliverance from Error*), written late in his life, al-Ghazali states that it was his habit from an early age, to search for the true reality of things. Going through a period of doubting his senses, and reason itself as means to certain knowledge, he went through a stage of deep scepticism during which he confessed to being a Muslim only verbally. In 1095, he left his material possessions and Baghdad to travel to Damascus as a wandering Muslim religieux. He gave himself up, as he says, to 'seclusion and retreat, spiritual exertion and struggle' in his attempts to purify his soul. He vowed never again to serve the political authorities, although he did, towards the end of his life, return to such teaching. Al-Ghazali went to Mecca to perform the *hajj* pilgrimage and, a year later, returned to Tus where he founded a small private school and a Sufi convent. Here he surrounded himself with Sufi disciples living an almost monastic communal life. Although he was lured back to teaching at the Nizamiyya college in Nishapur for a while, he died in 1111 in Tus, the place of his birth.

TURNING TO SUFISM

Al-Ghazali writes that he was delivered from his scepticism and spiritual crisis with the aid of the divine light, which helped him recover his trust in reason. Having such intellectual disorder in his life meant that he could not simply *think* his way out of this abyss. Using reason, he examined the teachings of 'the seekers after truth': the theologians, philosophers and Sufis. He studied much and complained that the philosophers considered their way of knowing by 'demonstrative proof' as being superior to theological knowledge drawn from revelation and its rational interpretation. For

1096–97

'The Revival of the Religious Sciences'. (*ihya` `ulum ad-din*)

1111

Al-Ghazali briefly returns to teaching and dies in his home town of Tus

al-Ghazali the primary evidence for God was not rational *per se*; there was no way to certain knowledge except through Sufism, through prayer and the development of the inner life, a virtuous life. This meant devoting oneself to rituals of the faith, to prayer and mystical practice. He was a philosopher himself, and used Aristotelian logic. But he also used philosophical principles to highlight the limitations of philosophy.

AL-GHAZALI'S WRITINGS

While most of Al-Ghazali's works are in Arabic, there are a few in Persian, of which his most famous is the *Kimiyayi sa`adat* (*The Alchemy of Happiness*), his own shorter version of his magnum opus, *The Revival of the Religious Sciences*. In *The Alchemy of Happiness*, al-Ghazali begins by writing that 'He who knows himself is truly happy'. Self-knowledge exists in realizing that we have a heart or spirit that is absolutely perfect, but that has been covered with dust by the accumulation of passions derived from the body and its animal nature. The essence of oneself is likened to a perfect mirror that, if polished, would reveal one's true divine nature. The key to this polishing is the elimination of selfish desires. As al-Ghazali writes, 'the aim of moral discipline is to purify the heart from the rust of passion and resentment until, like a clear mirror, it reflects the light of God'. This state of genuine happiness is not something most people attain, because ordinary mortals are so distracted by a desire for physical and earthly pleasures to remedy the pain of their souls that they have lost the ability to see the unseen. It is our enslavement to desire that causes our unhappiness.

Remember death

In *Letter to a Disciple*, al-Ghazali writes of Hatim al-Assam, who said, 'I observed mankind and saw that everyone had an object of love and infatuation that he loved and with which he was infatuated. Some of what was loved accompanied him up to the sickness of death and some to the graveside. Then all went back and left him solitary and alone and not one of them entered his grave with him.

So I thought and said, the best of what one loves is what will enter one's grave and be a friend to one in it. And I found it to be nothing but good deeds. So I took them as the object of my love, to be a light for me in my grave, to be a friend to me in it and not leave me alone'.

Al-Ghazali's greatest work, *The Revival of the Religious Sciences*, is a work that spans some 40 books. It has inspired scholarship and popular piety throughout the generations for successfully combining orthodox Sunni theology with Sufi practice as a guide to almost all areas of life and death. His purpose is to show how the doctrines and practices of Islam can serve as the basis of a profound devotional life, leading to the higher stages of Sufism or mysticism.

Accept an invitation

Al-Ghazali wrote that a person should not decline an invitation because of distance or because of the host's poverty or lack of social standing. He wrote that a distance that can normally be endured should not cause one to abstain. He wrote that the sacred books say, 'Walk a mile to visit a sick person, two miles to take part in a funeral, three miles to accept an invitation and four miles to visit a brother in God'. Precedence was given to accepting an invitation and paying a visit because it is through these that one fulfils the right of the living, who are more deserving than the dead.

Al-Ghazali's writing is rich and poetic, but also extremely accessible. He is one of the few writers to give a systematic account of love between God and man. He describes the mystical states and stations towards God by concluding that the love of God is the highest in rank and the last stage in drawing towards God before repentance and patience. Love is not a means to God, love is the end station, for the acquisition of the love of God is the end. As he puts it:

The ultimate rule of perfection of the servant of God is that the love of God most high triumph in his heart, so that his totality is engulfed (by that).

The condensed idea
Everyone should read al-Ghazali

43 Christianity

Islam arose after Christianity and spread rapidly in Christian lands. Christianity dominated the Near East and the Christian world received this new religion with curiosity as well as hostility. Until then, Christianity had defined itself against Judaism and classical paganism, but in the seventh century, Islam was to become its greatest challenge.

Christians are never named directly in the Qur'an, but are included, along with Jews, within the group of people whom the Qur'an calls the People of the Book (*ahl al-kitab*). Another general term denoting both Jews and Christians is 'scripturaries'. The one name that is used some 14 times in the Qur'an, in reference to Christians, is *nasara*, the Arabic form of the name Nazarenes, meaning those people from Jesus's home town of Nazareth, in Galilee.

There has been much scholarly speculation as to who the Christians are that the Qur'an speaks about, and which Christian group is being referred to specifically as the Nazarenes. Some scholars claim that, from the latter part of the fourth century, the term 'Nazoraeans' is used by Christian authors in order to designate heretical sects that, in modern theological literature, are usually called Jewish Christians. The usual Syriac word for 'Christian' is *kristyān* (pl. *kristyānē*). Mary or Maryam is also mentioned more times in the Qur'an than in the entire New Testament. As Jesus's mother – a chaste and virtuous woman – Mary lives in daily piety within many Muslim and Christian communities.

TIMELINE

8TH CENTURY CE	1492	16TH CENTURY
John of Damascus (d. 749) pens first Christian response to Islam	End of Muslim rule in Spain	Martin Luther (d. 1546) sees Muslim advance in Europe as an apocalyptic sign

THE PERCEIVED THREAT OF ISLAM

Much doctrinal polemics and apologetics in the Christian–Muslim debate have continued to focus on how God is understood *as* revelation and also *through* revelation. Both religions recognize that there can be no adequate account of human experience without reference to God. However, many Christian writers of the East placed Islam in the broad context of a monotheistic belief but critiqued the religion for its misunderstanding or denial of Christ's salvific status. Islamic monotheism was welcome, but most Christians writing about Islam saw this emerging faith as a powerful threat to Christian lands.

> **IF WINGED WORDS COULD HAVE CARRIED ME IN THEIR FLIGHT UP TO THE SKIES, I'D BE SEATED NOW IN THE HEAVENLY SPHERE WHERE THE PROPHET JESUS IS.**
> Khushal Khan Khattak, (1613–89)

One of the first people to engage with Islam and its doctrinal heresies was John of Damascus, a Christian monk and priest of the eighth century and one of the last fathers of the Eastern Orthodox Church. Most Christians who learnt of Islam recognized that the oneness of God formed the very basis of Muslim monotheism. But if unity in the Trinity was the most confusing aspect of Christian doctrine for Muslims, the Qur'anic message of divine unity was derided by Christians, because Muhammad's claims about prophecy and scripture were deemed to be false. For notable Christians engaging with Islam throughout history, it was Christological doctrines that distinguished Christianity from other faiths and any religion that did not recognize the divinity and redemptive work of Christ was a false religion.

The person of Jesus is central to the history of Christian–Muslim engagement. The source of all the controversy around Jesus in Islam, is to be found in the Qur'an itself. While Islam is the only religion outside Christianity in which Jesus is really present, with the epithet *ruh-Allah*, or 'spirit of God', the Qur'anic story of Jesus is of Jesus the prophet, not Jesus the Messiah.

19TH CENTURY	2001 ONWARDS	2014
Western missionaries aim to convert Muslims to Christianity	Events of 9/11 in New York lead to a renewed emphasis on interfaith dialogue	Islamic State empties Iraqi city of Mosul of its indigenous Christian population, for the first time in two millennia

> Christ Jesus, the son of Mary, was no more than messenger of Allah and his word that he bestowed on Mary and a spirit proceeding from him. Say not three it will be better for you Allah is one God. (Q4:171)

Such verses were understood to confirm the humanity of Jesus and the Christian doctrines of the Trinity and the Incarnation were rejected by Muslim theologians. Yet despite doctrinal debates about Jesus, Christians are described in the Qur'an as humble and given to seeking asceticism and knowledge:

> Nearest among them in love to the believers will you find those who say, 'We are Christians', because among these are men devoted to learning and men who have renounced the world, and they are not arrogant. (Q5:82).

CHRIST THE SAVIOUR

Much of the dialogue relating to Christianity has been based on verses that speak of Jews and Christians in the context of salvation:

> Those who believe and those who are Jewish and Christians and who believe in Allah and the last day and work righteousness, shall have their reward with the Lord, and on them will be neither fear nor will they grieve. (Q2:62)

Here, it is belief in God and the Last Day that is emphasized as that which distinguishes believers from unbelievers. For those who seek commonalities between the two religions, such verses are a path to a greater understanding of God.

While theologians debated doctrines, some Muslim poets offered alternative images for Jesus and Christianity. For the 13th-century Persian poet Rumi, Jesus is less saviour and Son of God and more the Muslim prophet. Yet Rumi sees Jesus as the smiling prophet and much more than a miracle worker. As a prophet, Jesus represents the perfection of humanity, a concept in which the attributes of God are manifest.

RELIGIOUS CONFLICT

There have been many conflicts between Christian and Muslim civilizations throughout history. The recent conflict in Syria, and in many parts of the Middle East, which has witnessed sectarian Sunni–Shi`a killing, has also compounded Christian–Muslim tensions, as Christians have increasingly become targets of Islamic State and its anti-Western Muslim sentiment. Christian churches and communities have been attacked, and while there are stories of Christians and Muslims protecting each other as ancient neighbourly communities, the escalation of violence against some Christian communities has created a new political tension that inevitably plays out in the West's image of Islam as a whole.

No cross in Islam

Islam has no image like the cross. Christian views of the cross vary, but for many Christians, it represents Christ's broken body and a brutal death. Yet in Jesus's death, eternal death is wiped out.

The German-American theologian and commentator Reinhold Niebuhr (1892–1971) said that Christianity is a religion transcending tragedy, for the cross is not the tragic but the resolution of tragedy. The Indian Muslim philosopher Muhammad Iqbal, for whom Christ held no special status, although he called Christ 'the lamp of all creation whose light lit up the world', held a very different view. Iqbal fundamentally disagreed with the basic point of orthodox Christianity, 'No religious system can ignore the moral value of suffering', but 'the error of the builders of Christianity was that they based their religion on the factor of suffering alone, and ignored all the other factors'.

Yet many Muslim poets used Christ as a symbol of healing and hope. The 18th-century Urdu poet Mir Hasan, for example, reflects the widely held view of the asceticism and spirituality of Christ, 'If Jesus lives in heaven, it is because, for years, he roamed the desert lands of love'.

The condensed idea
Christians are 'nearest in friendship' to the Muslims

44 Judaism

The Qur'anic reference to Jews and Christians occurs 31 times in the phrase *ahl al-kitab*, 'People of the Book'. While this phrase has connotations of family and a religious community who all received a divine book, the Qur'an sees the Jews as the chosen people but who failed to keep their covenant with God.

Historians state that there is evidence of a Jewish presence in South Arabia towards the end of the fourth century and that, by the sixth and seventh centuries, there was a considerable Jewish population in the area of Hejaz and mostly around Medina. Jews, along with Christians, are a recognized community of believers in the Qur'an. But while Jews, Christians and Muslims share a common vocabulary as monotheistic religions, the Qur'an paints a varied picture in its references to the Jews.

PROPHETS OF THE PAST

A fundamental link with the Jews is through multiple references to past prophets. What the Qur'an conveys is an overriding sense of continuity found in the repeated mention of the names of Old Testament prophets. But the Qur'an does not quote earlier scripture directly, even though biblical resonances are to be found in the Qur'anic text. The concept of prophecy is shared between Judaism, Christianity and Islam, even if the stories of the prophets diverge in their moral messages. Moses was perhaps the first to define the phenomenon of a prophet as one who claims to speak with divine authority, although it can be traced much further back in the history of God's people. The Qur'an states that, 'To every people we have sent a messenger, that they may worship God', to

TIMELINE

622–632 CE	1135–1204
Muhammad and early Muslims live with Jewish tribes in Medina	Jewish scholar Moses Maimonides lives under Muslim rule; and writes in Arabic

draw attention to the universalism of prophecy as being God's chosen method of conveying his divine message in human history.

JEWS IN THE QUR'AN

It is commonly accepted that Jews and Muslims share a similar monotheism, and there are several Qur'anic references to the Jews. However, recent scholarship claims that it is very difficult to know to which Jewish communities the Qur'an is referring. The references could be to rabbinic Jews, but also messianic groups. This emerges through a particular verse, 'the Jews say that Uzayr is the son of God and the Christians say the Messiah is the son of God' (Q9:30).

> ❛ WHAT YOU YOURSELF HATE, DON'T DO TO YOUR NEIGHBOUR. THIS IS THE WHOLE LAW; THE REST IS COMMENTARY. ❜
>
> Rabbi Hillel
> (110 BCE–10 CE)

While there are many references to Christians believing in a 'son of God', this verse could be understood as both messianic Jews and Christians believing in the Messiah as the son of God, but calling him by a different title – Jews calling him Uzayr and Christians calling him Messiah. As Moshe Sharon writes in his essay entitled 'The People of the Book', such Jews 'should not be equated with post-exile Judaism, which had categorically rejected any association with Jesus'.

The most common types of verse addressing the Jewish people express a plea to the Jewish people or a recognition of their belief in God:

> O children of Israel! Call to mind my favour which I bestowed on you and that I made you excel the nations. (Q2:47)

> Surely those who believe, and those who are Jews, and the Christians, and the Sabians, whoever believes in God and the last day and does good, they shall have their reward from their Lord, and there is no fear for them, nor shall they grieve. (Q2:62)

1948

Creation of
the state of
Israel; first
Arab–Israeli war

1948–70s

Massive Jewish
exodus from Arab
Muslim countries
to Israel

Muslims, Jews and the law

Law is central to the ways in which Muslims and Jews think and practise their faiths. Both Islam and Judaism are considered religions of the law: *shari`a* and *halaka*, respectively. But the law is complex in both religions and is tied to belief, ritual, interpretation and ethics.

Judaism upholds the covenant between God and the Jewish people through the written and the oral Torah. Rabbinic tradition worked in two principle ways. By imitating the sage, a disciple incorporated Torah into his very being. As an interpretative tradition for the meaning of scripture, rabbinic tradition was an intellectual commodity learned by studying and mastering the rabbis' oral teachings. In the wake of rabbinic Judaism, Judaism could no longer imagine the Torah without, at the same time, imagining the supplementary tradition of interpretation that spelled out the written Torah given to Moses. As Maimonides advises in *A Guide for the Perplexed*, the Torah is not a book of history or poetry, but a book of laws. If laws are bequeathed for all time, they cannot be read exclusively as an expression of one unique historical moment, but should rather be seen as an ongoing discussion between the divine and the human.

The problematics of law lie primarily in the fact that, in both Islam and Judaism, the outsider sees law largely through a prism of ritualism in opposition to the ethical. Law is the external, the public and the ceremonial, whereas true spiritualism or true morality is to be found in the internal and the unstructured. Muslims and Jews see observance as love for God.

In many verses, Jews are grouped with Christians – as well as other communities – as those who will be saved on the Day of Judgement, for their belief in a God and for having received a divine scripture. Yet alongside such verses are also those that have been interpreted as more exclusivist in tone as, for example, 'Who seeks other than Islam as a religion, it will not be accepted from him'.

The tension in many verses referring to the *ahl al-kitab* is that they are seen, on the one hand, as believers in the one God, but on the other hand, as those who have erred by rejecting Muhammad's prophecy and message. The multiple references to the Torah and the Gospel (*Injil*) make clear that what is being revealed to Muhammad was also revealed to the Jews and Christians in their books:

He has sent down upon you, [O Muhammad], the book in truth, confirming what was before it. And he revealed the Torah and the Gospel. (Q3:3)

Despite varying theological perspectives, both Jews and Christians had the status of *dhimmis* under the Muslim state, by which they had state protection in return for a tax called *jizya*. This allowed them to practise their own faith and have their own legal courts.

JEWISH-MUSLIM RELATIONS

The Qur'an speaks extensively about the Children of Israel (*Bani Isra'il*) and recognizes that the Jews (*al-Yahud*) are, according to lineage, descendants of Abraham through his son Isaac and grandson Jacob. Muslims share this ancestry to Abraham through Abraham's son Ishmael. Muslims also share common practices with the Jews, such as fasting and almsgiving, as well as abstention from eating pork, and observing other dietary laws – *kosher* in Judaism and *halal* in Islam. These are made manifest through the centrality of religious law in both religions: *shari`a* and *halaka*.

In 1948, with the creation of the state of Israel, the Arab states declared war, but were defeated. Subsequent wars between the Israelis and the Arab states, as well as uprisings by the Palestinians, which combine both religious and nationalist rhetoric, have weakened Jewish–Muslim relations. Nevertheless, there are many interfaith groups all over the world who strive for greater reconciliation and peace between the two religions and their communities.

The condensed idea
Jews are both favoured and admonished in the Qur'an

45 Pluralism

Pluralism has become a focus of theological, social and political debate, a central point in our discussion of civil societies, often crossing boundaries of gender, race and religious minorities. Some Muslim scholars claim that the Qur'an contains a divinely ordained pluralism that respects religious and cultural difference as well as freedom of conscience. Others argue that Muslim societies struggle with secular democratic pluralism, the hallmark of modern liberal societies.

Much of the discourse around pluralism within Islamic thought is less concerned with any systematic Qur'anic exegesis than it is with a selection of verses in the Qur'an that have been used to argue for an inherent Qur'anic endorsement and ideal of pluralist societies.

The verses are used by scholars to argue that religious and, therefore, civil pluralism is not an ideal, but is the only social and political framework envisaged in the Qur'an for good societies. Verses commonly used as a defence for religious pluralism are:

> O humankind, we have created you male and female, and appointed you races and tribes, that you may know one another. Surely the noblest among you in the sight of God is the most God-fearing of you. God is all knowing, all aware. (Q49:14)

TIMELINE

651/652 CE	13TH CENTURY
Uthmanic codex	Sufi poet, Jalal al-Din Rumi promotes inter-faith harmony

For everyone of you, we have appointed a path and a way. If God had willed, he would have made you one community so that he may try you in what he has given you. So compete with one another in good works. (Q5:48)

INCLUSIVIST VERSUS EXCLUSIVIST

In defending an inherent pluralism of thought within Islam, contemporary scholars such as Abdulaziz Sachedina state that religious pluralism for the sharia was not simply a matter of accommodating competing claims to religious truth in the private domain of individual faith. Rather, it impacted on public policy so that a Muslim government had to 'acknowledge the divinely ordained right of each person to determine his or her spiritual destiny without coercion'. Therefore, we can find many periods in history when Muslim states acknowledge the rights of non-Muslim citizens to practise their faith and to live by their own religious laws.

> ❝ A SOCIETY IN WHICH PLURALISM IS NOT UNDERGIRDED BY SOME SHARED VALUES AND HELD TOGETHER BY SOME MEASURE OF MUTUAL TRUST SIMPLY CANNOT SURVIVE. PLURALISM THAT REFLECTS NO COMMITMENTS WHATEVER TO THE COMMON GOOD IS PLURALISM GONE BERSERK. ❞
>
> John W. Gardner,
> On Leadership (1912–2002)

Scholars also invoke the Prophetic state in Medina as the first example of civil society in which duty, law and obligation bound people to one another, as an ideal point of reference from which to extract certain principles. Others refer to the *dhimmi* rules that, under Islamic law, ensured legal protection for religious minorities living under Muslim rule.

Politically, much has rested on an individual Muslim government's understanding of religious pluralism. Alongside such verses quoted above, are also those verses that have been interpreted as more exclusivist in tone – for example, 'Who seeks other than Islam as a religion, it will not be accepted from him'.

1908	2014
Mirza Ghulam Ahmad writes *A Message of Peace*	Conversion from Islam to another religion illegal in 23 Muslim countries

Liberal democracies

It may be that liberal democracies have lulled us into thinking that we in the West are now living in the best of all possible worlds, as such democracies have gained almost universal legitimacy. This is the view of the American political scientist, Francis Fukuyama. In a thesis entitled *The End of History and the Last Man*, Fukuyama states that the liberal *idea* rather than liberal practice has become universal.

He argues that no ideology is in a position to challenge liberal democracy. He also argues that, although Islam constitutes a coherent ideology with its own code of morality and political rule, 'this religion has virtually no appeal outside those areas that were culturally Islamic to begin with'. As Fukuyama contends, we may want peaceful lives, but as individuals we are mostly restless and passionate beings, in search for causes. We are always looking for a struggle, because our primordial instincts are restless.

Fukuyama has argued, powerfully, that even if the world was 'filled up' with liberal democracies, so that there is no more tyranny or oppression, people will find their struggle against some cause, because they will struggle for the sake of struggle. They will struggle, in other words, out of a vain boredom, for they cannot imagine living in a world without struggle. This means that, if the greater part of the world is characterized by peaceful and prosperous liberal democracy, then they will struggle against that peace and prosperity, and against democracy.

In writing about the verses that advocate tolerance and acceptance of other people, many scholars lament that, despite a clear message of universality, tolerance and pluralism in the Qur'an, the universalist and inclusivist dimension of the Qur'an, and the Islamic tradition more broadly, have been deliberately trumped in favour of the more exclusivist verses. This has been done in a bid to uphold Muslim religious superiority and to exercise undue control over the lives of minorities in Islamic countries.

TOWARDS A CIVIL SOCIETY

But pluralism means more than religious pluralism. Today, in most Western societies the political language is that of liberalism and liberalism speaks a language of rights through which the individual is at the centre of the world view; liberalism recognizes and celebrates individual choice, because it recognizes the individual over the collective. This has given a new model of freedom to society, along with a new social order in which religion no longer retains its former elevated position. The rise of democratic rule, the concept of civil society, the consciousness of all kinds of human rights – especially for minorities, including gender rights and sexual rights – are all part of this new political and moral consciousness. Here, concepts of human dignity and democracy are emphasized as integral to pluralist societies. Thus, irrespective of East or West, the human rights language, including its international dimension through the 1948 Universal Declaration of Human Rights, has captured our imagination and immersed itself in the global political and legal discourse.

Our present consciousness of civil societies in an increasingly globalized world, demands that it be based and developed on an intellectual and social acceptance of diversity, because in the modern period it is only within civil society that different standards and moralities can live side by side in relative harmony. One could say that, while diversity is not inherently a good thing, cultural diversity allows us – at times commands us – to compare and contrast value systems and different lifestyles so that we can move towards building more universal values and beliefs.

Pluralism is the political and social paradigm of the West, but it faces the challenges of rising religious fundamentalisms. Many Muslim countries still do not share the same level of religious pluralism or tolerance that most Western countries have established over the last few decades. There are many reasons for this, but pluralism should be seen as an aspiration. It is not a state of being, it is a constant process that needs negotiation and commitment from lawmakers, policy makers and all those who have a stake in creating peaceful civil societies.

The condensed idea
We should never take peaceful societies for granted

46 Multiculturalism

In essence, multiculturalism is a socio-political project that recognizes and accommodates religious and ethnic diversity within the wider nation state.

The origins of British multiculturalism are partially rooted in South Asian migration, which rose as the demand for manual labour increased during the post-war reconstruction. Since these migrants were generally employed as factory workers in large cities, they lived together in crowded multiple-occupancy homes and this eventually brought about a sharp separation between native and immigrant communities. Skin colour and the relatively lower socio-economic conditions created an atmosphere of racism and discrimination against many of the newly arrived immigrants. A number of anti-discrimination laws of the 1960s were significant for their tackling of racism, but much of the legislation focused on race and there was a noticeable lack of policies to combat religious discrimination.

MUSLIMS IN WESTERN SOCIETY

Most western European countries have experienced a similar level of multiculturalism from immigration over the last 70 years. Many claim that multiculturalism has brought diversity and enriched Western societies. In recent years however, there has been a rising critique that multiculturalism, especially the Muslim component of it, has failed, leading to isolationist cultures contributing, in turn, to radicalization of a growing number of youth. While recent scholarship shows multiple facets of multiculturalism, the process itself is tied to a particular kind of migration story, the successes and

TIMELINE

1950s–60s	1989	2011
Large-scale immigration from former colonies India, Pakistan and Bangladesh to UK	Publication of Salman Rushdie's *The Satanic Verses*	UK prime minister, David Cameron, says 'state multiculturalism has failed'

failures of which are only now becoming apparent. If 30 years ago, multiculturalism was defined through food and festivals, today it is examined through the prism of terror and human rights. The question has become one of values, especially in relation to the diverse Muslim presence in the West.

Britain, France, Germany and the Netherlands have different ways of accommodating and regulating immigrant communities and their religions, including Islam. They do, however, share one thing and that is a common anxiety in the way Islam is represented as an individual or collective voice, and how its public religiosity conflicts with the privately Christian, publicly secular otherness of liberal Europe.

> **NEW YORK IS ONE OF THE GREATEST CITIES IN THE WORLD. IT IS A FITTING HOST TO ITS MANY INTERNATIONAL VISITORS, WHO CAN COME TO WITNESS FIRST-HAND WHAT A VIBRANT MULTICULTURAL DEMOCRACY LOOKS LIKE.**
>
> Ban Ki-moon (b. 1944)

SELF-EXPRESSION

Muslim societies have been under a political spotlight since the crisis over Salman Rushdie's *The Satanic Verses* in 1989. The book was considered blasphemous by some Muslims and led to a fatwa calling for Rushdie's death by Ayatollah Khomeini, then supreme leader of Iran. This incident was one of the first to show book- and effigy-burning Muslims, whose actions also brought into focus the debate about freedom of expression.

The debate about Islam and rights of self-expression came into focus again in 2005 with the Danish Cartoon crisis in which the Danish newspaper *Jyllands-Posten* published 12 cartoons of Muhammad. Many Muslims claimed this was an insult to the Prophet and a direct attack on Islam. The riots, protests and violent demonstrations that accompanied this publication, led Western commentators to claim that the Muslim reaction reflected a clash of values, and that certain minority communities did not share the values of liberal democracies and civil societies of the West.

2014

The right-wing, anti-Islamist 'Pegida' movement is head-quartered in Dresden

2016

British referendum on membership of the EU; immigration a central issue of the campaign

The UK is still Christian

In 1997, the historian Peter Clarke made the observation that, in the 20th century, Great Britain lost its historic identity as a Protestant nation. But how do we measure a nation's religious identity? Notwithstanding declining church membership or diminishing formal worship, Great Britain is still largely Christian, if by that we mean the dominant faith of the land. Institutional religion has declined as a cohesive force giving meaning and stability to communities or, as Charles Taylor put it, 'religion has lost its public hold'. But our calender, our formal occasions, our legal system, our social and literary reference points, our cultural memory – all of these are still largely rooted in the context of Christianity. These are the factors that keep Christianity alive as a social force, even if the doctrines, rituals and beliefs are becoming increasingly elusive to younger generations.

A FAILED EXPERIMENT

In September 2001, a date invoked simply as 9/11, the attacks on the World Trade Center in New York were seen as a direct conflict between the Muslim world and the West. This tragedy not only led to the American invasion of Iraq, but it marked the beginning of the war on terror as a domestic and international policy.

After the bombings on the London transport system on 7 July 2005, the rhetoric around the 'war on terror' rose to new heights. These bombings were seen not just as the aggressive face of home-grown militancy among young people who practised the Muslim faith, but more disturbing evidence of the failure of multiculturalism. The simple question on the lips of many has been, 'Why have so many in the Muslim communities failed to integrate in wider society and why are they so against the West?'.

More recently, in 2015, the attacks on the French weekly satirical newspaper, *Charlie Hebdo*, saw 12 people killed, including cartoonists and the publishing director, Charb (Stéphane Charbonnier). Once again, this event raised the question of liberal Western values being under threat from an extremist form of Islam, which many claim is a direct consequence of the failed multicultural experiment. The question many ask is whether Islam and the Muslim world can ever accept and respect the notion of civil, diverse societies in which there are competing moralities and divergent discourses, and in which criticism and self-criticism are fundamental to healthy democracies?

While academic research shows mixed attitudes to multiculturalism – many claiming that it has not failed and that most minorities are loyal to Britain – the political narrative is one that calls for a more integrated cohesive society. Politicians such as David Blunkett, Jack Straw and David Cameron have called for greater articulation of the common values that underpin British democracy. This has translated into debates about citizenship and, since 2002, citizenship education has become a statutory subject for children from 12 to 16 years old. Since January 2004, individuals who successfully naturalize as British have to undergo a citizenship ceremony during which they give an oath of allegiance and a pledge of citizenship.

The UK is also secular

Religion, with all its complexities, continues to be a central feature of human life, giving shape and meaning to our existence. But this is often lost in the media attention given to contesting whether religion is a force for good or bad in the modern world. The concern is not so much about private religion, but about the possible reach of religion in the public space. Here, religion is often seen as something that drags us back to an intolerant past, whereas secularism grounds us in individual freedom and pulls us towards a hopeful future. Secularity as a process has been successful.

SHARED VALUES

Underlying all of these measures is the assumption that people in Britain no longer have a clear sense of common values, and that there is no longer a shared 'British identity'. This purported decline of a shared sense of Britishness is often attributed to the effects of immigration. But what we are debating is not so much Britishness, but a liberal set of ideals prevalent in much of western Europe – freedom of expression, rule of law and respect for religious freedom. These are the aspects of Western culture that are being challenged by the complexities of multiculturalism. And, by this, most people mean only the Muslim component of multiculturalism.

The condensed idea
There is no alternative to coexistence

47 Jihad

A central, yet controversial concept in Islam, jihad has become a well-known term in the West owing to its association with Islamic radicalism and terrorism. For this reason jihad is often understood as 'holy war'. More specifically, the basic meaning of *jihad* is to 'struggle' or to 'strive'.

This struggle has been conceived in many different ways within Islam, including, but not limited to, a military struggle against unbelievers. *Mujahid* (pl. *mujahideen*) is the Arabic term for 'someone who struggles', or a 'participant in jihad'. The importance of the concept of jihad in Islam has led to many Muslim scholars describing it as the 'sixth pillar of Islam' (see also, Chapter 22).

THE LANGUAGE OF JIHAD

The Qur'an frequently uses the language of jihad along with the expression 'in the path of God'. The 'path of God' here refers to the path of right conduct and belief that is laid down in the Qur'an and Prophetic *sunna*. Jihad occurs in a variety of contexts in the Qur'an. In some verses it refers to the individual's personal struggle towards God. This includes the struggle of performing regular prayers, fasting or the *hajj* pilgrimage (see Chapter 25). In other contexts the language of jihad even refers to the efforts of unbelieving parents to force their children to renounce their faith in Islam. Elsewhere jihad is used to indicate a military struggle, although this is not the most frequent term to denote violence or war in the Qur'an, with the term *qital*, meaning 'fighting', being more common.

TIMELINE

622–750 CE	10TH–17TH CENTURIES
Early Muslim conquests; Islam spreads to Spain and Central Asia	In later Sufi tradition, 'greater jihad' usually understood as battle against the self

THE GREATER JIHAD

The central importance of jihad in Islam can be illustrated by citing a famous *hadith*, whereby the Prophet is reported to have declared upon returning from battle, 'We have returned from the lesser jihad to the greater jihad'. When asked what constitutes the greater jihad, he replied, 'It is the struggle against oneself'. This lays out the famous distinction in Islam.

The greater jihad is internalized as a spiritual and moral struggle, a process of honestly and critically engaging the self. The lesser jihad involves physical battle against enemies and unbelievers. Many Muslim scholars recognized that persistently and patiently trying to improve oneself for the sake of God was a much harder challenge than a simple death on the battlefield. Implicit in describing jihad as the sixth pillar of Islam is the recognition that this is also a never-ending struggle. The religious life is ultimately one of constant struggle and self-improvement for the sake of God.

The distinction between the greater and lesser jihad became particularly influential in Sufi mystical thought. Sufi thinkers understood the greater jihad as the daily battle against selfish desires and worldly temptations. These threatened to lead the believer away from the disciplined, religious life. On this note al-Ghazali famously declared, 'Never have I dealt with anything more difficult than my own soul, which sometimes helps me and sometimes opposes me'. Al-Ghazali compared the human body to a city that was governed by the soul and besieged by man's lower, base instincts. He portrayed man's battle against his own selfish desires as the greatest battle facing the believer, yet also as the necessary means of gaining spiritual insight and intimacy with the divine (see also, Chapter 42).

> **WE NEED TO PRESENT THE ARAB AND MUSLIM WORLDS WITH A BETTER VISION THAN THE APOCALYPTIC FANTASY OF THE JIHADISTS – A VISION OF PEACE, PROSPERITY, TOLERANCE AND RESPECT FOR HUMAN DIGNITY.**
>
> Bill Richardson (b. 1947)

19TH CENTURY	2001
Muslim thinkers like Muhammad Abduh write of 'defensive jihad', based on just-war theory	Post 9/11, jihad now commonly understood as individual or collective militant action

The modern jihadi

Civil war erupted in Syria five years ago, and now President Bashar al-Assad's government, Islamic State, an array of Syrian rebels and Kurdish fighters all hold territory. Millions have been displaced and more than 250,000 people killed as a result of the fighting. But one of the most curious and alarming aspects of this conflict is the number of people from the UK (estimated at over 700), who have travelled to Syria to support or fight for jihadist organizations such as Islamic State.

Flag of the Islamic State

In November 2015, one of the most famous of these militants, named Jihadi John, was killed in a drone strike according to the Pentagon. Jihadi John's real name was Mohammed Emwazi and he was a Kuwaiti-born British militant. He had grown up in the UK, travelled to Syria and subsequently appeared in videos of the beheadings of Western hostages, including British aid worker David Haines and taxi driver Alan Henning.

While many considered him a barbaric murderer, others thought he was simply a pawn in Islamic State's game. There was also some concern that, despite his own murderous activities, he should have been tried in a court of law.

HOLY WAR

In the West, jihad has become a code word for holy war. The word came to prominence during the end of the Afghan war in 1989. But since then, violent extremist groups are commonly described as jihadi groups, because Islamic State or al-Qaeda describe and justify their actions through the rhetoric of jihad.

In so doing they draw on a central Islamic concept, conferring religious legitimacy upon themselves while portraying themselves as defenders of the faith who are undertaking a religious duty. Many scholars highlight how the practices of these groups represent a clear break with the juristic precedents and conditions of the past, however. The killing of non-combatants, the use of premeditated suicide as a weapon of war and the targeting of women, children and even fellow Muslims as collateral damage is better understood as a radical break from the classical jurisprudence on military jihad, rather than a faithful expression of it. The word jihad thus carries many different meanings for Muslims today.

A PERSONAL STRUGGLE

The most famous understanding of jihad as holy war is not only erroneous, but not a meaning that touches the daily lives of ordinary Muslims. Most Muslims understand jihad as a personal or spiritual battle in trying to lead a pious life, rather than a military or political struggle. Yet what is most notable is how this diversity and nuance often lends itself to calculated misrepresentations and polarization of the term. This misrepresentation occurs when an offensive violent 'holy war' is presented as the only possible meaning of jihad because of the actions of militant groups. Yet to deny that jihad can also mean warfare is also erroneous.

Jihad is a central concept of Islamic doctrine, but precisely because it justifies the use of arms and the upsetting of established rulers, the Muslim jurists always tried to limit its application so that it did not become a simple tool for sedition and killing amongst unauthorized individuals.

The condensed idea
Tragically, the word jihad is now an English word

48 Political Islam

Political Islam has no single definition, either in lay or academic circles. It is used loosely to refer to both 20th-century revivalist and modernist movements across the Muslim world, as well as ideological trends considered radical and neo-fundamentalist among a growing number of Muslim youth. To some extent, political Islam or Islamism in all its manifestations, contains several paradoxes, including overthrowing existing states and institutions and reinterpreting Islam for contemporary challenges, as well as promoting particular notions of Islamic principles in society.

In contrast to Muslims who wish to practise their faith indifferent to their political surroundings, Islamists are explicitly politically engaged in critiques of those institutions and practices that do not conform to their views of an ideal Islam. While they are heterogeneous in their outlook and there are overlaps both complex and subtle between Islamist and non-Islamist groups, Islamist movements are often characterized by social conservatism, literal readings of the foundational texts, the Qur'an and *hadiths* (see Chapter 35), strong emphasis on Islamic ritual and dress and, most importantly, the notion that salvation is tied to participation in this world. Political Islam often calls for the implementation of Islamic law, or sharia, which is perhaps the defining feature of Islamist movements (see Chapter 36). Western observers often distinguish between Islamist groups and the personal piety, beliefs and practices of ordinary Muslims, which is considered simply Islam. Yet this distinction is anathema to Islamists themselves, who consider their views a representation of true Islam.

TIMELINE

1949	1967
Hassan al-Banna, founder of the Muslim Brotherhood, assassinated in Egypt	Six-Day War between Israel and Egypt, Jordan and Syria

THE RISE OF ISLAMISM

Political Islam emerged as a dominant movement across much of the Islamic world in the early part of the 20th century. Some see this rise of Islamism as a reaction to Western cultural, political and military dominance, and particularly the West's engagement with the Muslim world through European colonial rule. Others point to the experiences of oppression under dictatorial secular regimes in the Arab world, continuing economic stagnation in many Muslim countries or the widespread sense of Arab humiliation after defeat in the Six-Day War with Israel in 1967. For many, the Iranian Revolution of 1979, which turned Iran into theocratic government, is the closest that political Islam came to succeeding. Others point to the growing role of Saudi Arabia using its enormous oil wealth to export its particular brand of Wahhabi/Salafi Islam since the 1970s.

These reasons need not be exclusive. Whatever the specific reasons, Islamist groups seek to address popular grievances and restore a

Whither Turkey?

There is a growing debate in Turkey as to whether the country is becoming more Islamic or more secular under the rule of Recep Tayyiph Erdogan's presidency and the AKP party. Some argue that Turkey's secular social, educational and legal order is under serious threaten from the rise of a political Islamism. Many observe that God's role in politics has been rekindled. Instead of continuing with the democratic software of tolerance and pluralism, there is fear that everything now hinges on whether people are pious or not. In many ways, the course of Turkey's republican history is testimony to the best kind of democracy emerging from an Islamic country, but political Islamists are jeopardizing secular education so that education is becoming more Islamicized. Segregation between the sexes is also increasing, because Islamists define social morality in terms of a woman's virtue. Others argue that an increasing authoritarian rule and an overtly Islamist narrative does not mean that Turkey will become 'another Iran'. Despite the ambitions of religious elites in the state, Turkish society is based on a deeper and more complex dynamic of identity, technology, urbanization and capitalism. Thus, liberal values and religious belief will continue to coexist in a relatively relaxed manner because that is what most Turkish people want, despite the attempts from various bodies to preserve Turkey from what they see as Western cultural imperialism.

1979	2001	2011
Iranian revolution and overthrow of Western-backed Shah of Iran	9/11 terror attacks in New York	Arab Spring uprisings; new democratic openings opened for Islamist movements across the Arab region

sense of Muslim empowerment and superiority through the political implementation of their Islamic vision. The call to implement sharia is held as the solution to modern ills. But this is not a return to any classical heritage of interpretation, but rather a reimagining of society in which early precedents, such as the Prophet's leadership in Medina, or the expansion of the Islamic Empire under the early Muslim leaders, are held as historical proof of the superiority of Islamic faith over other systems of governance.

ISLAMIST THINKERS

Several key ideologues have been instrumental to the growth and world view of Political Islam. The Egyptian Hassan al-Banna (d. 1949) was the founder of the Muslim Brotherhood. Under mottos such as 'the Qur'an is our constitution' and 'Islam is the solution', al-Banna sought Islamic revival through preaching and by providing basic services to his Egyptian community. Al-Banna believed in the gradual implementation of Islamic law, as a means of eliminating colonial influence in Egypt and the Muslim world. In South Asia, Sayyid Abu Al-a Mawdudi (d. 1979) held that Muslim society could not be truly Islamic without governance by sharia. He accepted Western notions of universal human rights, which were being formulated and ratified during his time, insofar as they did not contradict Islamic law. The Egyptian thinker Sayyid Qutb (d. 1966) has become particularly famous in the West owing to his posthumous influence upon radical groups like al-Qaeda. Qutb became the leading figure of the Muslim Brotherhood after the death of al-Banna. Qutb famously declared:

> THE ISLAMIC EXPERIMENT IS A HUMAN EFFORT THAT MAY SUCCEED IN SOME COUNTRIES AND FAIL IN OTHERS, AND THE RISE OF MUSLIMS IN POLITICS IS A HUMAN EXPERIMENT THAT IS NOT ABOVE CRITICISM.
>
> Salman al-Quda (b. 1955)

Islam is not simply a creed to be preached to the people by pronouncements. It is a comprehensive and manifest path, representing a liberating movement to free all of humanity.

The idea of Islam as a 'comprehensive path' means there can be no separation between politics and religion. For Qutb, sharia alone could guide Muslim society. He described both Muslim and non-Muslim societies, as currently living in a state of *jahiliyyah* – a Qur'anic term denoting the historical period of pre-Islamic ignorance, yet one that Qutb reinterpreted as a universal condition arising wherever Islamic law is not enforced.

ISLAMISM FOR THE MODERN DAY

Since the end of the Cold War, many in the West see Islamist groups replacing communism as a new threat to the West. Islamism is now increasingly seen as synonymous with terrorism. However, contemporary Islamism is not a monolithic movement, and there is great diversity across the range of Islamist groups. Questions concerning gradual or revolutionary social change, democracy, the primacy of sharia and the attendant rights of religious minorities or women, intellectual freedoms, all elicit different responses from various Islamist groups. There are clear differences between the Islamist *Ennahda* party in Tunisia, which has engaged with secular opposition and rejected many controversial aspects of sharia, and the Islamic State movement in Iraq and Syria. However, it is commonplace to put both groups under the broad banner of political Islam.

The democratic openings that emerged after the Arab uprisings of 2011 have ushered in a decisive period for Islamist movements. Across many countries, such as Libya and Tunisia, Islamist parties have risen to prominence as the primary beneficiaries of democratic elections. For movements that have spent most of their history in opposition, these successes create new possibilities, but also unprecedented challenges. Many question the capacity of Islamist groups to address long-standing, systemic issues of poverty, unemployment, economic development, gender inequalities, corruption and illiteracy that plague much of the Muslim world. Perhaps their biggest challenge lies in the appeal of the modern Western world and whether any Islamic vision can offer a meaningful alternative.

The condensed idea
Religion and politics are never far from one another

49 Militant Islam and IS

From the events of 9/11 to the more recent attacks in Brussels, Paris and the Charlie Hebdo killings, Islam has invariably come to be seen as a religion that is inherently linked with violence and intolerance. Radical organizations such as al-Qaeda and, more recently, Islamic State threaten global peace and continue to polarize the Islam/West debate.

One of the key features of militant Islam is the practice of *takfir*, which loosely parallels as 'excommunication'. *Takfir* involves accusing other self-declaring Muslims of unbelief. Militant groups are often described as *takfiri* groups. In the classical period, accusations of *takfir* were extremely restricted. The sole evidentiary criterion was usually an open confession of unbelief by the accused. Classical Islamic thinkers like al-Ghazali (d. 1111; see Chapter 42) generally held that all who declared the *shahada* remained Muslims, no matter how deviant their other beliefs or how sinful their practices. Such scholars also recognized the possibility of ignorance on the part of the believer, and thus *takfir* was rejected until it was established that clear teaching and guidance had been given. Among radical groups today, however, these traditional restrictions on *takfir* no longer apply. Radical *takfiri* groups characteristically view themselves as alone possessing religious truth; and thus rejecting their message is equated with denying the Prophet Muhammad and God.

TIMELINE

Sept 2001	March 2003	July 2005
9/11 attacks in New York	Invasion of Iraq by American and coalition forces as part of the 'War on Terror'	7/7 bombings on London's transport system

AN ISLAMIC CALIPHATE

Although militant Islam entered the Western consciousness primarily through the actions of Osama bin Laden, al-Qaeda and the events of 9/11, the group known as Islamic State (IS) has emerged from the chaos of the Syrian civil war as the most recent form of radical Islam. This group is commonly called *Daesh* in Arabic; an acronym of *al-Dawla al-Islamiya fi 'al-Iraq wa al-Sham,* which translates as The Islamic State in Iraq and the Levant (ISIL). Territorial expansion and military successes were reflected by the group later dropping geographical specificity and simply calling itself the Islamic State (*al-dawla al-islamiyya*).

On the first day of the month of Ramadan in 2014, the group took the historic decision of announcing the creation of a global Islamic caliphate. No other extremist group had previously taken such a hugely symbolic step. The declaration of a caliphate means that the group now proclaims itself the legitimate representative for all Muslims worldwide, restoring a political institution that harks back to the time of the earliest Muslim rulers. This declaration also implies a desire to continue to advance until it has conquered all Muslim-majority lands, an aspiration frequently expressed in jihadist maps of a unified Islamic empire. This makes the Islamic State group both a political and theological threat. It embodies a hard-line *takfiri* theology that has acquired a large swathe of territory and is seeking to build and develop real state infrastructure.

> **EVERYBODY'S WORRIED ABOUT STOPPING TERRORISM. WELL, THERE'S A REALLY EASY WAY: STOP PARTICIPATING IN IT.**
>
> Noam Chomsky (b. 1928)

The Islamic State group has taken militant Islam into new, unchartered territory in many other ways. Chief among these has been the introduction of a powerful eschatology into IS propaganda. The Qur'an itself makes frequent reference to a final Day of Judgement, and IS propaganda is replete

May 2011	**June 2014**	**Jan 2015**
Death of Osama bin Laden by US Special Forces	Islamic State seizes control of Mosul; Abu Bakr al-Baghdadi announces creation of a 'caliphate'	*Charlie Hebdo* terror shootings in Paris

Women joining jihadists

A curiously alarming phenomenon of the rise of Islamic State is its appeal to young Muslim women and girls. Hundreds of Western women have left their homes in Western countries to join Islamic fighters in the Middle East. Girls as young as 14 or 15 are travelling mainly to Syria in the hope of becoming 'jihadi brides'.

Counterterrorism experts claim that they are being recruited, some say groomed, via social media. Many are drawn to the promise of a devout jihadist husband, a new home in a true Islamic state which is presented as a contrast to living in the land of the infidel. Most of all, they are made to believe that they will be serving God and their religion by fighting alongside their male jihadists and bearing children so that Islamic State can grow.

Even if most women jihadsts serve a fleeting purpose, they are lured for the same reasons as men. These women go against the stereotype of the oppressed young woman and see their actions as women taking agency for their own lives. They have chosen to leave the comfort of their Western homes to help the Islamic State fighters.

Female Islamists, even violent jihadists, have long been prominent. In 2010, Afia Siddiqui, a neuroscientist from Pakistan, was found guilty in New York City of attempted murder of US personnel investigating her material support to al-Qaeda. In Pakistan her radicalization was honoured with the title 'Daughter of the Nation'. She is now serving an 86-year sentence in federal prison.

with apocalyptic descriptions of the impending 'end times'. Current battles in Iraq and Syria are seen as portents leading to a final apocalyptic battle between Muslims and the unbelievers.

This can be seen in the significance the group places on the town, *Dabiq*. *Dabiq* is the name of IS's English-language magazine, and refers to a small town near Aleppo in northern Syria where, according to one *hadith*, Muslim and Christian armies will finally face each other and the crusaders will be destroyed. The *hadith* from Abu Hurairah states that the Prophet is reported as saying,

'The last hour would not come until the Romans would land at al-A'maq or in Dabiq. An army consisting of the best (soldiers) of the people of the Earth at that time will come from Medina (to counteract them)'.

ANTI-SHI`A SENTIMENT

Islamic State have also introduced sectarian, anti-Shi`a rhetoric into militant Islamism. The group has particularly targeted the Shi`a as a key part of their brutal onslaught, as it considers Shi`a Muslims to be apostates. This differs from other militant groups such as al-Qaeda, which primarily target the West, specifically Western global hegemony and its influence and interference in the Muslim world, and indeed even stress Muslim unity in the face of this threat. Frequent media reports tell of Islamic State fighters capturing groups of people and releasing the Sunnis, while withholding the Shi`as for execution. This has infused modern militant Islam with a new violent sectarianism, in turn giving rise to sectarian tensions in many parts of the Muslim world.

The Islamic State group has taken militant Islamism into a new, and more barbaric phase. Of most concern for many in the West is the group's appeal to a small but significant number of Western Muslims. The group's propaganda openly reflects a dichotomous world view, dividing the world into two camps of Islam and *kufr*, or unbelief. In this divide, Muslim communities living in the West form a 'grey zone' that the group candidly states it wishes to eradicate. The message is that you are either with the caliphate, or the forces of unbelief. Recent IS-orchestrated attacks in the West have had the inevitable, but unfortunate consequence of increasing Western fear and suspicion of local Muslim communities, which are often seen as harbouring secret loyalties to Islamist groups.

The condensed idea
Militant jihadism is seen as the biggest global security threat

50 Democracy and human rights

There is an increasing concern among Western scholars and policy makers that Islam poses a threat to the liberal, secular values of the West. Political theorists state that the re-emergence of certain types of religiosity in the public sphere threatens to destabilize civil societies and global orders.

Islam has gradually come to Western consciousness as a religion of another world, essentialized and archaic, often in complete disagreement with principles of secular democracies. This debate has a long history but a new urgency in our globalized world.

EARLY ISLAMIC RULE

There have been varied views as to whether the earliest period of Islamic rule exercised any fledgling democracy and to what extent some Muslim countries are democratic today. A popular argument is that the Qur'an contains principles of consultation, freedom and community consensus that negate autocratic power and that point towards some semblance of democratic rule. The claim is that the *shura* concept – a special form of consultation – formed a democratic basis in early Islam, and that this was the case until the period of the first four caliphs (known as the *Rashidun*) came to an end. Later Muslim philosophers, such as al-Farabi (c. 872–950), regarded the ideal state to be ruled by the Prophet instead of a platonic philosopher king. Furthermore, it is also argued that the religious freedom

TIMELINE

508–507 BCE	1215	1789
World's first democracy in ancient Athens	Magna Carta adopted by King John of England	Outbreak of French Revolution; calls of liberté, equalité, fraternité

that is fundamental to notions of democratic pluralism existed in classical Islamic law and gave Christians, Jews and other groups freedom to practise their faiths and laws.

DEMOCRATIC LIBERALISM

Yet, despite a long history of political theorists and religious scholars advocating that Islam and democracy are compatible, the argument today is not about the processes of democracy. Rather, the question today is one of values, not voting rights. On the one hand, political leaders in the Muslim world face revolts and uprisings, but have no interest in promoting liberalizing values. Secondly, Muslim societies in the West often seem reluctant to appreciate and accept the software of secular liberal democracies – not just democracies – which are based on pluralism, the rule of law and freedom of conscience.

TO DENY PEOPLE THEIR HUMAN RIGHTS IS TO CHALLENGE THEIR VERY HUMANITY.

Nelson Mandela
(1918–2013)

There is no doubt that, in most Western societies, the political language is that of liberalism and liberalism speaks a language of rights and celebrating individual choice, because it recognizes the individual over the collective. This has given a new model of freedom to society, along with a new social order in which religion no longer retains its former elevated position in society. The rise of democratic rule, the concept of civil society, the consciousness of all kinds of human rights, including gender rights and sexual rights, are all part of this new political and moral consciousness. Here, concepts of human dignity and democracy are emphasized as integral to human flourishing, even though these words remain contested in meaning and scope.

HUMAN FREEDOM

The human rights language, including its international dimension through the 1948 Universal Declaration of Human Rights and other

1948	1990
UN Declaration of Human Rights established (UNDHR)	Cairo Declaration of Human Rights in Islam in response to UNDHR

What rights are universal?

It is said that all countries apart from Saudi Arabia supported the 1948 Universal Declaration of Human Rights (UDHR). Some Muslim representatives raised their concern at the Western bias to the way in which the UDHR was formulated, which they saw as potentially conflicting with some principles of Islamic law. While there was agreement around the universality of the concept of human rights, there was disagreement on the specificity of which human rights were considered universal. In 1981, a number of Islamic countries came together to issue the Universal Islamic Declaration of Human Rights (UIHDR). The tone of this document was very different. It began with the statement that Islam had given humanity human rights 1,400 years ago. It focused on God as the principle lawgiver, 'Human rights in Islam are firmly rooted in the belief that God, and God alone, is the Lawgiver and the Source of all human rights. Due to their Divine origin, no ruler, government, assembly or authority can curtail or violate in any way the human rights conferred by God, nor can they be surrendered'.

The word for rights, *huquq* can also mean truth and was used to distinguish between rights or claims of man as opposed to the 'right of God'. However, scholars, such as the Egyptian reformist Sheikh Mahmud Shaltut (1893–1963) did not agree with this distinction. In 1990, Muslim countries including Iran and Saudi Arabia came together to present an 'Islamic' alternative to the UDHR and issued the Cairo Declaration of Human Rights.

conventions, has captured our imagination and immersed itself in the global political and legal discourse. However much the principles are contested, it is not just the concept of human rights but their universality that has gained momentum over the last few decades.

But this kind of rights-based language is either muted or a contested feature in many Islamic countries. In fact, modern Islamic states and societies lag far behind international standards of equality, democracy and human rights. For example, when it comes to religious freedom, many Muslim countries – while historically allowing people of different faiths to worship in accordance with their conscience – now limit this freedom to those outside of the Muslim faith.

There is no human dignity without human freedom. Today, freedom of religion, whether understood as an individual or collective right to practise a faith, to convert to another faith or to worship in public, is considered by many as a moral good that is indispensable in a community of free individuals. Although the Qur'anic verse, 'There is no compulsion in religion' (2:256) is seen as affirming human freedom, it remains controversial. And yet, it must be understood in the context of contemporary pluralist societies, not just as a theological abstract, but as the embodiment of normative judgements and ways of living that carry political and social resonance.

Reformers within the Muslim world recognize that pluralism and diversity are built on free expression. As Abdulaziz Sachedina said in *The Islamic Roots of Democratic Pluralism*, 'The term pluralism is one of the catchwords of a new world order, whose diversity of cultures, belief systems and values inspires both exhilaration at the endless shadings of human expression and dread of irreconcilable conflict. The invocation of pluralism has become as much a summons as a celebration, an urgent exhortation to the citizens of the world to come to terms with their dizzying diversity'.

Notwithstanding the huge diversity of Muslim rule and societies, there are certain values in Islamic thought and culture that either resonate with liberal humanism or can be reconciled with the moralities of a pluralistic age. The theological language of compassion (*rahma*) and justice (*adl*), and the spirit of intellectual inquiry (`*ilm*) have been part of the Islamic consciousness for centuries and can be reclaimed in a real sense to transform many parts of the Muslim world. Verses of empathy such as 'Had God willed, he could have made you one community' (Q5:48) and 'We have appointed you races and tribes so that you may know one another'(Q49:13) point to pluralism being a challenge and a good. Yet pluralism cannot simply be a matter of individual taste or preference; it needs to be institutionalized into the very structure of civil societies. Norms cannot be analyzed outside the structures of power or the specific embodied social practices in which they are embedded and expressed.

The condensed idea
Human rights are a struggle, not a given

Select glossary

Abraham
One of the most significant prophets in
the Qur'an. Precursor of Muhammad in
establishing the Kaaba and the pilgrimage
rites in Mecca.

Adam
The primordial human being, and the first
prophet of Islam. The name 'Adam' can also
be taken as a synonym for human beings in
general.

Allah
The Arabic word for God.

Caliph
Vicegerent of God. In the Qur'an, Adam is
specified as God's representative – a symbol
of the privileged status given to man by God.
Historically, a caliph was the head of the Muslim
state.

Fiqh
Islamic jurisprudence. The science of exploring
sharia law.

Five Pillars
The five foundational tenets that are
obligatory upon all Muslims: the witness to faith
(*shahada*), prayer, almsgiving, fasting
and pilgrimage.

Hadith
The sayings of the Prophet or those of his
companions concerning his activities. *Hadiths*
are gathered into a number of canonical
collections, the most famous in Sunni Islam
being Bukhari and Muslim.

Hajj
The annual pilgrimage to Mecca, which all
Muslims should try to perform at least once in
their lifetime, if possible.

Halal
Permissible and lawful according to the rulings
of sharia law.

Haram
Literally 'sacred' but in its wider sense, that
which is forbidden by sharia law.

Hijab
Literally meaning curtain or screen, now refers
to the Muslim head covering increasingly worn
by Muslim women.

Hijra
The word refers specifically to the Prophet's
migration from Mecca to Medina in 622 CE, and
the beginning of the Islamic calendar.

Iblis
The original name of the fallen angle. Iblis
became the 'accursed Satan' when he
refused to prostrate himself before Adam at
God's command.

Imam
In Sunni Islam, the person who leads the
communal prayers in the mosque. In
Shi'a Islam, the imams are descendants of the
Prophet and the rightful leaders of the
Muslim community.

Islam
Multiple meaning of submission to God
and peace.

Isra'
The night journey that the Prophet undertook to
Jerusalem. Alluded to in the Qur'an in chapter 17,
commonly called *surat al-isra*.

Jihad
'Struggle in the path of God'. In its most
general sense, jihad is the believer's inner
personal struggle. In it's more popular use today,
jihad refers to a physical battle against the
enemies of Islam.

Kaaba
The black-and-gold draped cube called the
'House of God' and holiest sanctuary in Islam,
in the Sacred Mosque in Mecca. It marks the
direction of daily prayers.

Kafir
An unbeliever.

Kalam
Speculative Islamic theology.

Madhhab
A school of jurisprudence. In Sunni Islam, there are four schools: Hanafi, Shaf'i, Hanbali and Maliki. The majority of Shi`a follow the Ja`fari school.

Madrasa
A religious school or place of study, traditionally affiliated to a mosque.

Masjid
A mosque or place of prostration.

Mi`raj
Literally, 'ladder'. The ascension of the Prophet Muhammad to God. A major event in Muslim religious history.

Muhammad
The last of God's messengers and the recipient of his revelation – the Qur'an.

Muslim
One who submits to God and one who formally belongs to the Muslim faith.

Qur'an
'Recitations'. The word of God revealed to the Prophet Muhammad by the angel Jibril (Gabriel).

Ramadan
The ninth month of the Islamic calendar in which Muslims are required to fast daily from sunrise to sunset.

Salat
The five-times daily prayers that are one of the five pillars.

Shahada
The testimony of faith and first pillar of Islam, 'There is no God but God and Muhammad is the messenger of God'.

Shari'a
Literally, the 'road leading to water'. The divine law that establishes the prohibitions and commands of the religion. Based on the Qur'an and Prophetic *sunna*, alongside other sources such as scholarly consensus (*ijma*) and analogy (*qiyas*).

Shi`ism
One of the two main sects of Islam, making up approximately 15 per cent of the global Muslim population.

Sunna
The way of living and acting established by the Prophet.

Sunnism
The larger of the two major sects of Islam. Around 85 per cent of global Muslims.

Takfir
Branding someone a non-Muslim, effectively excommunication.

Tawhid
Divine unity. The affirmation of God's indivisible oneness.

Zakat
Almsgiving. One of the five pillars of Islam.

Index

First published in the UK in 2016 by

Quercus Edition Ltd
Carmelite House
50 Victoria Embankment
London EC4Y 0DZ

An Hachette UK company

Design and editorial by Pikaia Imaging

Edited by Anna Southgate

A CIP catalogue record for this book is available
from the British Library

HB ISBN 9781784296124
EBOOK ISBN 9781784296131

10 9 8 7 6 5 4 3 2 1

Printed and bound in China

Picture credits:

7: Crown Prince via Wikimedia; 19:
King Eliot via Wikipedia; 26: Tab59
via Wikimedia; 43: Youssef9055 via
Wikimedia; 45: ©Photo Researchers/
Mary Evans Picture Library; 91: Zied
Nsir via Wikimedia; 126: Steve Evans
via Wikimedia; 154: Arild Vågen via
Wikimedia; 155: Julia Kostecka via
Wikimedia; 159: Prakash Subbarao via
Wikimedia. All other pictures in the
public domain.